Introduction

D0637878

My name is Fraser Hay, and I stay 60 miles north of Aberdeen, and 14 miles past the back of beyond in the highlands of Scotland. Before I arrived on Linkedin, I had already generated over 400 **testimonials** on the UK's oldest social network and made £10,000 ($15,000) from a client who I've never met, residing in a country that I've never visited, which has a language that I can't even speak.

I connected with him online via a social network, and that was only the beginning.

That was over 10 years ago, and I've learned and documented a heck of a lot since then, and in this book, I'm going to share some of the juicy stuff I've learned and achieved in the following pages. You have in your hands, a very **practical** guide that will get results and help you to generate leads for your products, services and solutions every week – if you **apply** the contents. Stand by to start making a radical change to the way you manage your sales prospecting and the results you get from it. How many leads would you like to generate next week?

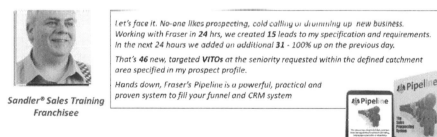

Sandler® Sales Training Franchisee

Let's face it. No-one likes prospecting, cold calling or drumming up new business. Working with Fraser in **24** hrs, we created **15** leads to my specification and requirements. In the next 24 hours we added an additional **31** - 100% up on the previous day.

That's **46** new, targeted **VITOs** at the seniority requested within the defined catchment area specified in my prospect profile.

Hands down, Fraser's Pipeline is a powerful, practical and proven system to fill your funnel and CRM system

In this book, I want to introduce you to the acronym and sales prospecting system of **P.I.P.E.L.I.N.E.** that can be successfully used to generate results on Linkedin. Many of the approaches you will want to test and evaluate and shock yourself as to how practical and powerful they are and what you can achieve in a very short period of time by making small, subtle changes the way you go about your prospecting and filling your pipeline.

When you see this symbol throughout the book. Pause & Reflect. Make notes, Answer the Question or Complete the exercise. This will greatly assist you.

Just reading and reflecting on the content will have little effect on the results you generate with your social networking on Linkedin.com until you convert these "thoughts" into action by applying them. Sorry, but it's true. I can lead a horse to water, but I can't make it drink.

INCREASE YOUR ROI

At the end of the book, I am going to invest in you to greatly save you time, energy and money with your online prospecting and filling your sales pipeline. As a thank you for investing in yourself and buying this book, I've got a wee surprise for you to help fill your pipeline and achieve a greater ROI – even faster.

To mentally prepare you for growing your network and filling your pipeline, you're going to need to change the way you manage your prospecting and selling online.

Stop thinking "features" and "benefits" and start recognising exactly what frustrates, exasperates, and stresses your market and prospective customers.

You need to know what pains, needs and problems they have, so you can empathise with them and demonstrate that you "understand" them, and can solve their problems, needs and frustrations.

To mentally prepare to improve your prospecting and filling your pipeline, you're going to need to change the way you manage your marketing and selling online. Stop thinking "features" and "benefits" and start recognising exactly what frustrates, exasperates, and stresses your market and prospective customers.

EXTRA BONUS

If and only if you do enjoy the book, and do follow the links, watch the videos, and apply the tactics, recommendations, strategies and techniques I share, would it be ok to leave a positive review for the book? For if you do, I have a couple of extra bonuses for you as a thank you, that I hope will bring you more pre-qualified leads and sales online.

You need to know what pains, needs and problems they have, so you can empathise with them and demonstrate that you "understand" them, and can solve their problems, needs and frustrations. You're going to go the extra mile by sharing valuable information with them. And like most relationships, you need to "communicate" better, and "listen" better. You need to explain and demonstrate that you are "listening" and are serious about wanting to develop a long term relationship. **Remember, Givers Gain, Takers Drain and Lurkers simply remain the same.**

I wish you well with your sales prospecting and filling your funnel, pipeline and CRM system.

You never know just how big your pipeline could grow.

Regards

Fraser J. Hay
January, 2018

Copyright Notice & Disclaimer

© Fraser J. Hay, 2018

All rights reserved. No part of this book may be reproduced in any form or by any electronic or mechanical means including information storage and retrieval systems – except in the case of brief quotations in articles or reviews – without the permission in writing from its publisher.

The figures you calculate are not a guarantee of earnings. These are intended to express your opinion of earning potential. No guarantees or warranties are made that you will achieve these results.

Your future performance is down to you, your attitude, your choices, your behaviours, and your consistent ability to read, relate, assimilate and apply prospecting tactics – daily.

Table of Contents

Part One – The Basics

The rules have changed

Prospecting – from offline to online

In addition to tele-canvassing, direct mail, advertising and attending tradeshows, business networking has been a popular method of prospecting and generating referrals for years.

Here are some more definitions of networking....

"People caring about People"
"What goes around, comes around"
"An organised way of creating links and opportunities with, and for people"
 "Giving and contributing to others, and asking nothing in return"

One site I recommend you use for business networking online is www.Linkedin.com; you will discover how networking can actually mean a whole lot more and can become an acquired skill for both social and commercial settings. More importantly, it can be used to fill your pipeline – fast.

The way it used to be

Traditionally, individuals would network, swap business cards, or meet old and new acquaintances at the following places:-

   Chambers of commerce
   Exhibition
   Trade show
   Business Club
   Local breakfast club
   Local authority
   A "networking" event

One of the major paradigm shifts in doing business in the 21st century and doing business online, especially when it comes to online networking is to SHARE.

Share your knowledge and expertise
Share your opportunities
Share your contacts
Share your skills

The whole ethos of our approach to prospecting and networking online is about sharing.

The more you share, the more people will want to recommend you, to others. Referral rates of over 25% have been reported by members.

There is a high referral rate, because people's personal networks begin to overlap, and people very quickly begin to recognise and know mutual acquaintances that could benefit from the services offered by a particular individual.

If that person is well known and liked, then the word of mouth (or word of mouse) will spread even quicker, increasing their awareness and exposure within the business network on the site.

400,000,000+ (yes, 400 million) Professionals from hundreds of industries are actively searching the extended networks of their trusted business contacts on Linkedin.com to discover inside connections to potential business partners, to get in touch with industry experts for advice, or to find recommended professionals to fill open job positions, or fulfill contracts.

A quick tip before we begin…

Consider adding the word "Unlike" at the start of your profile summary. Why?

It immediately sets out to differentiate you from others in your industry, sector or field.

Think about it. People who are visiting your profile will probably have visited your competitors, your peers and other people like you in the same industry so ensure you stand out by telling your profile visitors why you are NOT like them. Think how you could adapt your profile to do this.

For example, the start of my current LI profile reads –

"Unlike many business coaches, I've helped entrepreneurs from 44 countries to identify & address over 2000 common small business issues, challenges & obstacles that have been holding them back & preventing them from achieving their entrepreneurial goals & objectives.

Each of these issues have been documented and shared in my books on Amazon, my webinars, keynotes, workshops and coaching programs.

I offer no prescriptive advice, but best of all - Progress is measured, documented & guaranteed.

Can I help you?

Maybe. Maybe not.

Yes, if you want to:

• *Acquire new entrepreneurial skills*
• *Document your model, vision or strategy*
• *Increase exposure or position yourself as an expert*
• *Generate more leads, enquiries, sales or referrals*
• *Add new revenue streams & improve cash flow*
• *Grow Your Business®"*

Does your profile summary help to explain what you offer and for whom? More on this later.

Stop committing mal-practice

In order to achieve the breakthroughs you crave, you need to start by identifying why your prospecting on Linkedin.com isn't generating the results you want.

If anyone tells you differently, then they need their head examined.

Let me explain.

If you went to a doctor and he simply prescribed some medicine without first diagnosing you and clearly identifying the problem – he'd be struck off for mal-practice, and never work again in the medical fraternity. Worse, he could be sued!

The same is true when it comes to social media marketing and marketing in general, so many gurus and egotistical "wannabes" simply want to "prescribe" what they've just watched in a 2 minute YouTube Video and dish out their new found "prescriptive" advice and "expertise" without actually asking any questions or endeavouring to get to the bottom of the problem for their clients.

Why? Because they haven't got the necessary experience under their belt! They haven't tested many different approaches, failed at them, analysed them or studied them in comparison to others they've tested over a period of months and found out why they didn't work.

You don't have to be #1, you just need to be "seen", to be active, to be helpful, and people will want to click your profile photo and read your headline to get them to want to click your profile and engage with you. You just need to know what other's issues, symptoms, problems and challenges are. You need to find out what their pain is, either individually or as a group and start engaging them and helping them by asking questions. You don't want to join a group and go in all guns blazing and do a "me, me, me." – Oh, and yes I've cocked up by doing that too in the early days. See, you have to learn from your experiences and <u>apply</u> that learning.

I include 24 fill-in-the-blanks headline templates for you to use later in the book, but the point I want to make here is stop prescribing in your advice to others until you've done some preliminary analysis or diagnosis of their situation or what the common problems, issues and challenges of your target market are.

I'm not trying to blow smoke up your "jacksie", I'm trying to help you make real progress and like it or not, it will require effort – a lot of effort, but you will make progress.

You need to know why your sales prospecting on Linkedin may not be working (if it's not working), so you can focus on what needs fixing. There's no point pretending otherwise, and I really want to help you. Ready?

Ask yourself the following questions to find out why. Answer YES or NO, and then add up how many NO responses you have. **You may want to revisit this list after your read the book and applied the principles and tactics that I share later.** In the meantime, ask yourself the following questions, add up how many "Nos" you have, and make a note of your score

Do you know what the first word in your Linkedin profile summary should be?
Do you have a means of monitoring your progress/results on Linkedin?
Do you have an established product offering for Linkedin?

Do you know what the top 5 frustrations are that your prospects have on Linkedin?

Do you know how you can solve these top 5 frustrations for your prospects?

Do you have a "content strategy" for Linkedin?

Do you have a strategy or game plan already created with Linkedin?

Have you uploaded a photograph of yourself?

Have you tested the professional Headline on your profile to improve engagement?

Have you personalised your Linkedin profile url?

Do you update your Linkedin status at least 3 times a week?

Do you post a blog on Linkedin Pulse more than twice a week?

Have you connected your blog to your profile or linked to your blog via your profile?

Have you created a Slideshare account?

Have you linked your Slideshare account to your Linkedin profile?

Are you getting found in page 1 of the GLOBAL search results?

Are you getting found in page 1 of your local country search results?

Do you offer a FREE Item of Value to build your list/qualify prospects?

Are you a member of a niche/industry specific Group?

Are you a member of at least 10 industry/niche specific groups?

Do you post in your groups at least once a week?

Do you know how to generate backlinks from Linkedin to your sales pages?

Do you know how to get more ENGAGEMENT from your fellow Linkedin members?

Have you included your telephone number on your profile?

Are you receiving more than 5 contact requests a day on Linkedin?

Are you receiving more than 10 profile views a day on Linkedin?

Do you appear in more than 50 global search results per day on Linkedin?

Your profile doesn't read like a CV does it?

Have you uploaded videos, a speaker kit or testimonials to your profile?

Do you explain on your profile why you are different other professionals like you?

Do you explain the different types of organisation and individuals that you can help?

Do you know how to post content in ALL your groups simultaneously?

Do you list and link to your book(s) and course(s) via your Linkedin profile?

Do you use live video streaming in your sales prospecting?

Now, having answered each of the questions above, add up all your NO response, to give you a final total, and make a note of your score.

Made a note of your score? If it's more than 5, then you've got a bit of work to do and I think what is shared in this book will help you if you apply it.

Now you're beginning to understand where I'm coming from, and fear not, I'm fairly confident we can address a lot of the points above in this book. And if I can't address them all, you can always follow the suggestions at the end of the book.

Whatever you do, don't forget to come back to this list of questions, after you've read the book in its entirety and <u>applied</u> what I share.

Go back through the list after you've read the book and re-score yourself, and I bet you'll already be making progress.

That's the power and proof of what I'm going to share with you…

…If you put it all into practice.

Now it's time to crack on…

Desire – The Engine of Change

Educate yourself about your needs and the needs of others

Whether it's to find a job, find a supplier, find customers, joint venture partners, find referrals or simply to make friends, you first need to educate yourself about your needs and the needs of others. Let's look at several key factors that you will also have to consider if you want to succeed in networking.

You need to think about your mindset, temperament and/or disposition with regards to networking, what you want to achieve from your networking endeavours & what you can offer the individuals and organisations you will encounter on your social networking journey.

Many people fear rejection, obligation, appearing too pushy, or in some occasions, appearing too weak, and each of these issues need to be addressed and overcome.

Therefore, it's very likely that the mindset of the majority of people on Linkedin.com may actually be hindering the development of their personal networks
.
So one of the first things, you should consider is adopting the right mindset.

Mindset for Success

Do not let fear get in your way. Many people are afraid of meeting new people, selling or presenting in front of others.   If you have never been involved in any sort of networking before, you will be free of self-judgment based on past successes or failures in your personal and professional life.

How others perceive you is important, but not as important as how you perceive yourself. If your fellow members recognise you as someone who always makes an important contribution, (be it online in the blogs, in the clubs, or offline at events, at meetings), then you will always be in demand.

You may not become an overnight success, but neither will you fail instantly or permanently. Just as your body requires healthy, nourishing food, so does your mind, and remember that although there are many things in your commercial and personal life you cannot control, you can always control your attitude and how you respond to different circumstances.

While your time and how it is spent may be subject to the demands of partners, customers and others, your mind is the one thing that cannot be controlled by anyone but you. Your time is your most important asset & needs to be managed very carefully, so spend it with people who share your desire to succeed on Linkedin.com. (**Not surrounded with negative people.**)

I'm of the opinion there are 2 types of people in this world – "**drains**" and "**radiators**". Linkedin is full of radiators and opportunities. Establish your own philosophy for success, and stick with it, regardless what the rest of the world does. (And try and avoid/stay away from the sewage.)
Many new people just starting in networking hesitate to approach friends or family, or indeed complete strangers. In fact it is estimated that only one in ten are actually comfortable in talking to strangers. This means however, that for the vast majority of people, it is their own misgivings fears and doubts that are hindering them.

Many of these same people will then hesitate once earning an income out of guilt for accepting money that gives them profit from a friend's purchase. It may be a self-esteem issue - fear of loss of their friends, of facing rejection, of being wrong - and the other conversations are simply 'smoke screens' for the real ego-related issues. You must be 100% happy, and confident with the product, service or opportunity you are promoting. If you're not, then you're not going to be able to convince others. Conversely, if you are confident, then by adopting the right mindset, you will be able to enthuse others, and simply relay the facts, features and benefits of what you have to offer, and how you can help others meet their goals and objectives.

30 reasons why people join Linkedin.com. What's your reason?

To find better quality B2B prospects
To generate better pre-quality B2B prospects
To fill their pipeline
To grow their network of contacts
To generate sales
To get a job
To generate referrals
To raise awareness of the skills they offer
To build their house list
To conduct market research
To improve SEO rankings & web presence
To pull traffic to their website
To hire new staff
To find JV & Channel partners
To position themselves as a Thought Leader
To find suppliers
To generate endorsements
To build your personal branding
To test headlines & messaging
To promote their Slideshare.net presentations
To build a following
To get found in your niche, vertical market or group
To meet like-minded people
To get advice and solutions to problems
To share knowledge, contacts and opportunities

Seek first to understand, then to be understood. Make a list of typical reasons why you want to connect with others on Linkedin.com. More importantly, make a list of the reasons why prospective customers should engage with you.

The Real Cost of Your Online Prospecting

A few quick questions…

Be honest with me and yourself!

Ready?

Here we go…

 1. How many hours do you spend each week online?
Go on think about it and write it down.

Seriously, how many hours do you spend on your laptop, pc or mobile device?

Write it down.

Done that?

OK Good.

 2. Now write down how much you charge for an hour of your time?
(Either calculate what you charge or what you currently get paid).

Go on write it down.

Done that?

Excellent.

3. Now multiply your answers from questions 1 and 2 to give you a new answer. (Either calculate what you charge or what you currently get paid).

Let's call this No 3. Go on write it down.

That figure is how much of your time you're investing in the management of your online and social media marketing — every week. A bit shocked?

(You should be.)

4. Now multiply the figure you achieved in 3 above by 4 to give you a monthly fee. Write it down.

…your last by no means, least…

5. Multiply your answer in 4 above (The monthly investment of your time) by **12** to give you an annual figure of what you're investing social media marketing.

Go on write down the figure that you calculated in 5 above.

WOA! Say that number out loud right now.

Say it again out loud – slowly.

Yup, that's how much of your time you'd be investing in online marketing unless you read this book all the way through, and apply the knowledge, suggestions, activities and exercises contained in the pages ahead.

You need to change the way you're managing your social media marketing.

You need to come up with a new plan.

**You need to make small changes and implement little steps –
every single day.**

…and if you do, you'll start experiencing real results in no time at
all.

Now you know how much your sales prospecting online is costing
you in real terms.

Let's look at what you need to do about it, and how you can
change the way you manage your prospecting online to start
generating real permanent, breakthrough results.

7 Reasons why Linkedin members won't buy from you – yet

The most common mistake made by the average person in social networking is that they waste time trying to "sell," manipulate, pester, and persuade prospects to buy. A lot of time and energy is devoted to activities that will inevitably lead to...nothing. You will generate more sales, referrals, mutual opportunities and expand your network with less effort, when:

You learn to focus your efforts on helping others

You stop thinking of prospective customers as prey, for you are not a big game hunter

You treat your prospects with respect, and are *respected* by them in return.
You offer something for **FREE** that is of value to your   intended prospect.
You start by making a list of potential targets, suspects or prospects.

Your Starting Point is Your Online Profile on Linkedin.

But first, you might want to read the following -

1. They don't know you or trust you.

Give them a reason to want to get to know you, and give them a reason to trust you. Testimonials can help. A Money back guarantee can help. Offering a FREE trial or download can help. Start raising your profile, and visibility by blogging, writing articles, networking, attending events, exhibitions, hosting workshops etc.

Be different. Offer something different. Stop offering features. Start offering real benefits. Do you empathise with your target audience, do you know the problems they have, and can you genuinely help them? Do you serve to help? Or do you serve to control? What tactics can you use to get people talking about you and referring you to others who need help in the area you specialise in?

2. They don't want what you are selling.

A toughie. If they don't want it - Don't push it. But if they need it, and they don't just recognise that they need it, think how you can demonstrate or prove the value you offer.
Think how you can allow them to come to the conclusion that they have a need for what you offer - for the cost in not acting or choosing one of your solutions will be much more expensive in the long run.

You certainly don't want to waste time and money going to appointments to drink their coffee, waste their time and yours if it could have been decided hours, days or weeks ago whether they were interested in what you have to offer or not, and whether they **need** what you offer or not.

3. They won't pay what you want to charge them

Again, this is simply because they haven't recognised the value you offer. Calculate and demonstrate the opportunity cost, or the real cost in not acting. Calculate and demonstrate the saving or efficiency you offer, and/or the inefficiency, waste or spiraling cost or loss in not working with you.

Try this - Write down how much you want to generate in sales in the next 12 months - go on, write it down.

Write down how much you want to earn in revenues in the next 12 months. Done it? OK, good, now write down what your annual revenue is now. Go on; write down what your annual revenue is now. Done that? Excellent.

Now subtract your second answer from the first answer.

That's how much you're losing or not generating now - How can you illustrate that point with your clients? More importantly, how are you going to generate those revenues you want? What's the plan for them, and what's the plan for you?

4. They just don't believe in you.

Then prove it. Demonstrate it. Give them reason to. Offer a sample, a puppy dog close - a FREE trial. See 3 above. Show them the hundreds of testimonials you have, or all the videos you have on You Tube, links to your previous blogs - so they can sample you, what you know, what you've achieved and what you believe in - People buy from people they like.

Your prospects want 3 things – Confidence, Progress and Results - so give it to them. Give them the confidence they crave - and that you can help them to achieve the progress and the results you offer.

Quite often they simply don't know what it is they want because they don't where they're at, or where they've been, and thus they don't know where they're heading.
So why not help them do that - it starts by building confidence in your prospect's mind so that they can start to make progress and know that by working together will lead to even bigger and better results. Allow them to experience the help, guidance and support you offer, and how much you go the extra mile in order to nurture the relationship.

5. The timing isn't good.

Reschedule. Plan in advance. Illustrate and demonstrate the cost in not acting now. Introduce scarcity, limited stocks, impending price increase, delayed delivery times in not acting - Ask "why" the timing isn't good - to draw out the real reasons or objections and not just the excuses.

Offer a discount to commit today, but accept delivery in 1, 2 or 4 months' time. Will the "timing" ever be right; will the cost of their pain increase in the meantime or interim? What was your answer in that little exercise in 3 above - how much of a gap is there where your prospects are now, and where they want to be, more importantly, do they know what they want and know how you can help them achieve it?

6. They recognise the value, but they don't have the budget/money

Remind them of the cost in not acting. Introduce a discount for prepayment. Offer Split payment terms. Offer a Finance option, a Lease option, subtract or take away some of the value you offer, for a lesser offer or lesser price.

Ask them on a scale of 1-10 how serious they are wanting to solve the problem, and how much they can afford to lose or continue to lose compared to the price you charge. Why not offer them a 100% return on their investment?

7. Un-Answered Questions

Un-answered questions prevent sales from happening, so draw out the questions in advance via a list of frequently asked questions on your website, pre-empt the questions during your presentation by saying "you're probably wondering….well, what we do is….", Un-answered Questions can be eliminated by identifying the un-asked questions, and answering them before the prospect even thinks of them.

Un-answered questions are usually a lack of product knowledge or more importantly, a lack of belief in the product or lack of research in your customer's needs. More importantly, what questions have you forgotten to ask about your prospects, to ensure you qualify them thoroughly enough, so you don't waste their time, and they don't waste yours?

 Make some notes, and reflect on what you've just read. Think what changes you might want to make with your Linkedin marketing.

Your Networking Funnel

Suspects are at the start of your networking funnel, these are the people that appear to be open to being approached, and have a profile with their full contact details added. These are the people that you want to target and meet the criteria of the prospect profile that we will discuss later. They don't know you exist yet, and there has been no prior contact with them or from them.

Connections are suspects who responded to your sales prospecting activities and want to get to know you better. They're like you, are curious about what you have, do and offer. They want to follow you and wish to be connected to you and receive updates from you. Whilst they may have read your profile, you may not have qualified them nor had a chat about how you can help them.

Prospects are the people who meet the criteria in your prospect profile and can help you reach your commercial goals and objectives. These are the people who have requested your FREE Item of value (more on that later), and agreed to a chat by phone, by skype or in person. They have confirmed that they are interested in what you offer, but haven't parted with any cash yet.

Clients are people who have invested in the products, services or solutions that you offer. They know you, like you and trust you.

Advocates are usually clients (but not always) they're openly promoting (advocating) you and your services to others in their network, and you are reciprocating. They are recommending you to others in the status updates, group chats, newsletters, videos and webinars.

Network Partners are the people you are having the most frequent contact with, and have a much higher level of mutual trust.

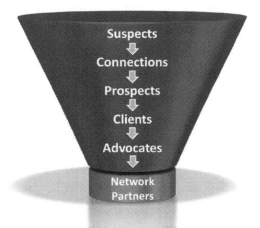

Building Relationships using your Networking Funnel _TM_

(Questions to use when approaching your fellow members)

What's the biggest project you're working on right now?
How can I help you?
Can you tell me a bit more about what you do?
Who do you know who might be able to help me with?
Who do you know who might be interested in?
If you were me, what would you do?
Who on Linkedin.com, would you recommend I speak to?
Where on Linkedin.com, would I find?
How would you like to proceed in taking the next step?
How can we make this happen?
How can we turn this into a win/win?
What do you recommend/advise?
Who would you recommend to….?
Who do you know that is an expert in this field?
Who do you know that is well connected?
What have you found to work well for you?

The above questions are simply guidelines to help you probe, enquire, and seek out the best ways to develop better relationships with all the people you have at the different stages of your network funnel. Your goal is to become better acquainted at each stage.

There are 4 very important things to remember when developing your networking funnel:

1. SELFLESSNESS

    Focus your attention on others – not yourself.

Selflessness

- Stop hunting and being out to see what you can GET
- Focus on giving on SHARING
- Offer different marketing items of value for FREE
- When you share useful content and ideas, people respond
- Other people are out to see what they can GET. You're not.

2. RESONANCE

    You will get more people in your network and pipeline who think and act like you.

Resonance

- People like people who are like them.
- People like people who think and act like them.
- People like people who are generous
- People like people who are helpful
- People like people who are focused on results

3.   FAMILIARITY

People respond better to people they are familiar with, so ensure you get seen (and heard)

Familiarity

- People do business with people they know, like & trust
- Join social networking groups online that your audience join
- On your online profile empathise with your target audience
- Participate in group discussions and answer questions
- Share your own experiences so others know you're "real".

4.   RECIPROCITY

No doubt about it – giver's gain ;)

Reciprocity

- People like to receive something of VALUE
- Those who receive also like to give something in return
- Learn to pay it forward and be amazed at what happens
- The more you give, the more you will receive
- More people you help, the more people they will refer to you

The single biggest mistake in sales prospecting and filling a sales pipeline

Yes you need to qualify people, but stop practicing "Selfish Prospecting" or "Selfish Marketing".

Quite often, prospecting for many small business owners just doesn't work, because they are trying to **GET** new customers...

All their energy and time is spent on trying to **GET** customers to work with them.

Ironically, by trying to **GET** new customers, your sales and marketing messages actually end up pushing them away...

Why is this case?

You probably **NEED** new customers and WANT more business. Yes?

Believe it or not, but this is reflected in all your prospecting activities.

- **It's reflected in your status updates, articles and group posts.**
- **It's reflected in your emails.**
- **It's reflected in your skype chats and on appointments.**

How many times have you gone to a networking event and met someone who you thought NEEDED the business?

How many times have you met people at networking events offline that you thought they were desperate for business? At networking events offline, how many times has someone given you a business card before you asked for it, and you never called them back? It's the same online.

What about when you keep reading status updates on Linkedin – "Buy from me. Buy from me."

You know what I mean. It happens all the time.

If you subconsciously are aware of this - **THEN SO ARE YOUR PROSPECTS**.

Your Prospects have a "Desperation" detector, and what's worse when you are in NEED of new business, you actually end up focusing on YOU - not the prospect.

Many small business owners don't realise it, but...

In all their marketing communications, emails, blog posts, article writing, and phone calls to previous clients it's all about THEM and WHAT THEY DO.

Worse still, they end up focusing all their marketing on what they KNOW, what they HAVE and what they DO.

They go into great detail about their products, services, and what makes them different. Don't you make the same mistake. For, by focusing on yourself, you become oblivious to everyone else and their pains, needs, wants and frustrations. Everyone else isn't interested in what you have, do or know, because they're preoccupied with their own problems, needs and wants.

They're pre-occupied with what <u>they</u> have, do or know.

Does any of this sound familiar?
- You're not getting the replies you want to your emails, articles or updates.
- You're leaving a lot of messages on voice mail.
- You're not getting the appointments from your follow-ups after those networking meetings.

If so, then you're beginning to think that prospecting online doesn't work.

You're almost right.

Selfish prospecting doesn't work well online.

Ironically, the more selfish prospecting you do, the more cynical and skeptical you become to social networking and social media marketing and end up convincing yourself it is a complete waste of time, and it begins to really affect your attitude not just to marketing but to doing business in general. You might get the odd phone call from an existing client that helps to stop the famine, but this feast and famine scenario is constantly repeating itself in regular sales cycles (or lack of sales) cycles.

…but there's good news.

You could change your approach, and begin to start generating INSTANT results.

For example
- Remind your prospects of their problems and how you can help
- Ask your prospects questions instead of talking about you
- Offer something for FREE upfront to demonstrate that you excel at what you do

More importantly, you could change your entire focus from GETTING to **GIVING**.

You need to start giving and sharing valuable advice, information and **"FREE ITEMS OF VALUE"** in all your sales and marketing communications online to help your prospects.

That way all your marketing activities are focused on the needs, problems and frustrations of your prospective clients - not **you.** Start offering valuable and useful information and resources to your prospects today.

Spend little or no time talking about you or what you **DO** or **HAVE**.

Remind your prospects of their pain, needs and frustrations, and they will become very interested in what you offer, for you offer a SOLUTION that can solve their problems.

Remember your Linkedin Profile should do all the qualifying. Your sales goal online is simply want to get people to visit and read your profile – that's it. More on that later.

At networking events offline, you shouldn't spend 5-10 minutes talking about **you** and what you **do**. You succinctly articulate what it is you offer, and then direct pertinent qualifying, fact finding questions to your prospect, to get them talking about what they KNOW, DO or HAVE.

You DO NOT want to rush to give people your card and have them dreading your follow up phone call the next day you will want to gently probe, enquire, and find out a little more about your prospect by asking good exploratory questions.

..and **if the answers they give you fit your criteria of an ideal prospect**, then

You will ask prospects for their card and tell them you're going to send them something for FREE in the next day or so, that will find of value and interest.

Guess what?
- They will now want to give you their card or personal details.
- They now look forward to your call.
- They will look forward to the FREE item of value you're going to send them.

Ensure you prevent becoming a victim of selfish prospecting online or offline.

Start offering **FREE** items of value. Start giving more value upfront**.**

You can also integrate this technique into your online, social and tele-marketing too, if you want to

If you're not generating the results you want from your sales prospecting online, then you're going to have to change your "M.O." – your modus operandi; the way you go about selling what you have to offer your target market. The secret is to be proactively helpful sharing good useful content, suggestions and ideas whilst reciprocating positively wherever and whenever you can.

Remember the mantra I shared in the introduction of the book? It's so true.

"Givers Gain, Takers Drain and Lurkers Simply Remain The Same."

Part Two – The System

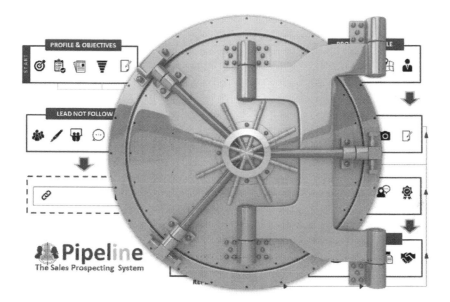

Profile & Sales Objectives

OUTCOME

By the end of this stage, you will have identified how many leads you need to give you the revenue you want and what your Key messaging should be.

Let's deal with your sales objectives first. So what do you want to achieve with your sales prospecting? You need to answer some fundamental questions regarding your business objectives. For example:

Turnover

How much turnover from your online activities do you want achieve in the next 12 months with?

Go on write it down.

Sales

How many sales do you need to achieve your turnover objectives above? Write it down.

Customers

How many customers do you want to achieve in your next 12 months? Go on, write it down.

Leads / Signups

How many leads do you need to generate the sales and revenue you want? If you're not sure then you need to write down what you estimate your closing ratio to be, for example 1 in 3, 1 in 5 or 1 n 10. You then need to multiply that number by how many sales you need.

For example, if you need 100 sales to achieve your revenue objectives and your closing ratio is 1:7, then you would need (100 sales x 7 = 700 leads.).

Connections

How many people do you want to have in your network(s) in the next 12 months? Write it down.

Signups / Downloads

Write down how many signups and downloads you want to achieve via your website in the next 12 months.

Subscribers

Write down how many newsletter or ezine subscribers you want to achieve in your next 12 months.

Members

Write down how many newsletter or ezine subscribers you want to achieve in your next 12 months.

Set Your Objectives For The Year Ahead.

 Ensure you have written down each of your objectives above (and any other objectives) that you wish to achieve for the year ahead.

Set Your Objectives For The Month Ahead.

Divide your Annual objectives by 12 to ensure you have written down each of your objectives that you wish to achieve for the month ahead.

Set Your Objectives For The Quarter Ahead...

 Divide your Monthly objectives by 4 to ensure you have down each of your objectives that you wish to achieve for the Quarter ahead.

Set Your Objectives For The Week Ahead...

 Divide your Weekly objectives by 4 to ensure you have down each of your objectives that you wish to achieve for the Week ahead.

In order to achieve these objectives, there are a number of activities you need to be doing daily or at least weekly on Linkedin as you work towards your goals and objectives.

These activities include:-

- Findimg and creating new connections.
- Viewing suspect's profiles
- Following up profile visits
- Posting updates
- Posting articles
- Posting and participating in groups.
- Giving endorsements

We'll cover this in more detail later in tbe book, but next, let's take a look at your profile.

Why Your Profile May Not Be Working

When it comes to your Linkedin profile, I'm not going to cover all aspects of your profile in this book. However, I will cover some very important factors. It starts why your profile may not be generating the engagement or requests for information that you would like. Address these 7 points and watch your conversions and engagement increase.

A. Not mentioning the Problems you solve

Are you forgetting to mention the problems you can actually solve for your target market in your online profile?

Your fellow members may actually be in need of your services, but if you don't tell them about the problems, pains or predicaments you fix, how will they know. How can they recommend you if they don't know what it is you actually fix or solve?

Some of your fellow online members visiting your profile may also be suffering from, or experiencing these problems, pains or frustrations. One of the first things you want a visitor to say when they visit your profile is - "Yup, I know how that feels" or "I know someone who knows how that feels".

People don't want to get to know you, if they don't think you can help them, or if they don't know what it is you do, or don't think you're **worth** getting to know.

 Make a note of the problems you fix, and add them to your profile.

B. Not describing the people you help

Do you actually mention who your clients are, the type of clients, and the criteria you look for in a client, on your profile?
The majority of people on forums and social networks are pretty vague in this respect, and then they wonder why they get all sorts of vague introductory emails from people they don't want to communicate with, more importantly, they receive pro-active communications from people who do not have a need for their products or services, and the profile owner reacts negatively of accusing their fellow member of being "spammy".

You are on a networking platform for god's sake; you are inviting people to contact you. All you have to do is start saying on your profile who are the people you want or need to contact you.

 Do you say who you help on your profile? Do you list the type of clients you work with and who could benefit from your help?

C. Forgetting to mention the solution you offer

It's funny, how many times have you visited a profile....Read about the person, their football team, their partner, children, which sign of the zodiac they are, which car they are like, even which character from the Matrix they are like, (some even do describe the car they are like) but you have no compelling reason or wish to actually contact them, because you don't know what problems they solve or whether they can actually help people like you. You need to discuss what can be achieved if people use your product or service and what things are likely to happen if people engage with you and their problems are solved - **create a desire or want for them to communicate with you.** People are interested in one thing only - results. Talk about the results you offer.

 Do you actually describe the solution you offer prospective clients on your Linkedin profile?

40

D. The Reason why

Have you forgotten to remind your fellow online members why your prospects and people you know, are experiencing the problems they are, and why they are stuck with the problems listed in **A**, and more importantly, not taking advantage of **C**. By explaining the reason why people experience the problems they do, you are further demonstrating you know your craft, have a thorough knowledge of your subject, and it helps to build to trust and credibility.

You need to explain why the reader might be having problems in your area of expertise, so you can disqualify them from being a potential client or not. Why do you think the same people keep revisiting your profile - they think you can help them, they're not just sure how or why.

 Update your profile to say why visitors and prospects should work with you and not your competitors.

E. You

We've touched on this earlier, it's about credibility and positioning you as an expert, not every aspect of your social and personal life to give scam artists and identity thieves everything they need to open a bank account in your name.

How many business meetings have you gone to, and asked the person sitting opposite you about their dog, or which character of the matrix they are most like. You simply don't do it.
Stay focused on what you talk about regarding yourself; build a profile about you and your achievements, your track record, the people you've helped.

Yes, give an introduction to who you are, but don't dwell on it or make the classic mistake of selfish marketing and do a "me. me. me" talking only about you and not the people you can help.

Update your profile to focus on the reader or prospect – NOT YOU.

F. How can they help themselves?

Stop going to meetings that lead to nothing. Stop visiting profiles and think oh she's nice, let's have a coffee. You need to describe the basic steps that readers of your profile need to take in order to help themselves (or further qualify or disqualify themselves). People are silently begging to be led, they want a solution, they think you can help (**if you've followed steps A-E**), but now what? How can you prove you can help them?

How can you help readers of your profile resolve their problems or at the very least, start making progress to give them confidence that they should in fact be speaking with you, want to meet you, or even engage you to provide a solution.

 Update your profile to tell your prospects and visitors to your profile how they can help themselves.

G. Next step

Ever had loads of people visit your profile that lead to nothing - no 121. No phone call. Not even a personal message to acknowledge they've read your profile and found it interesting. Do you actually tell your prospects what they should do next having read your profile. Remember **F** above?

People are silently begging to be led. They need your solution, they're just not convinced you should be the one to provide it - they need convincing, they need **Confidence** to know you CAN and WILL help them.

Start building that confidence by leading and demonstrate you can help them. Think. You've explained who you are, what you do, who and how you can help, next step is obvious - **Invite them to get in touch and CONTACT YOU.**

How much money do you think you might have lost, by not implementing any, some or all of the above?
It's time to stop having a wishy washy online profile.

You're running a business for god's sake.

 Update your profile to let your prospects and profile visitors what the call to action is and what they need to do next.

Focus on the NOW – not the past

Don't just sit and remember the good old days, when you had a "proper job" and a full expense account. Worse, don't focus on all your past achievements, if you're on Linkedin to win new business.

Personally and I know I'll get some flak for this, but I think that too many LI profiles focussed on the past instead of what one can do now or in the future to be assistance to prospective customers and clients.

More and more Linkedin profiles are appearing to read like CVs. That's all well and good, if you're looking for a J.O.B. Far too many B2B business owners, managers and self-employed entrepreneur's Linked profiles look like and read like CVS, and as a general statement, CVs tend to be just good records of previous employment.

Many small business owners are on Linkedin to win new business, create partnerships, grow their network and win advocates for the knowledge, talent, skills and results they can bring to the table - now. (But that's not how they position, present or sell themselves on Linkedin)

Yes, I appreciate some people are looking for jobs, and yes, recruiters are looking for candidates too.

Is a profile simply talking about all your previous jobs going to persuade potential prospects, partners and employers to want to engage with you NOW? Is it going to give sufficient reason as to when they should be doing business with you NOW or in the FUTURE?

Many members want to know what you offer NOW and how you can help them to reduce costs, increase efficiency, maximise profitability, improve their ROI for the FUTURE and the potential results you could bring to the table.

They want to know what they can GET if they engage with you.

Forgive me, for I may be wrong, but are prospective clients looking to find out which school you went to or which character of the matrix you are or do they want to know NOW what problems you can fix, who you can help, the solutions you offer and what they can expect if they choose to ENGAGE with you now or work with you in the future?

What do you think the focus should be on your Linkedin profile?

How do you think you can improve your Linkedin Profile to encourage others to engage with you? Well, let's do a forensic analysis of my profile, and see if you agree or not, (for it's working for me.) Ready, let's begin…

Forensic Analysis of a Linkedin Profile

Sorry, but I didn't want to adopt a herd mentality and follow everyone else in what they were doing on Linkedin, so let me explain what I've done. Hopefully it will make sense. You can always visit my profile directly at www.fraserhay.co.uk.

STEP 1 – Pull them in. Attract their attention; we covered this in the last section. Be different and encourage and entice those searching to want to click and visit your profile.

Fraser Hay
Founder of Grow Your Business®, author of 15 books on Amazon helping owners to achieve their entrepreneurial objectives
www.fraserhay.com • Entrepreneurial Skills at Grow Your Business School
Cullen, Moray, United Kingdom • 500+ &

STEP 2 – Time to introduce and credentialise myself, whilst adding a hint of realism in there too, in that I'm not promising the earth. Your prospective profile visitors are fed up of your competitors over promising, over selling and simply not being realistic. Don't make the same mistake as everyone else. Simply give them some quick facts about you and some of your achievements to date.

Unlike many business coaches, I've helped entrepreneurs from 44 countries to identify & address over 2000 common small business issues, challenges & obstacles that have been holding them back & preventing them from achieving their entrepreneurial goals & objectives.

Each of these issues have been documented and shared in my books on Amazon, my webinars, keynotes, workshops and coaching programs.

I offer no prescriptive advice, but best of all - Progress is measured, documented & guaranteed.

Can I help you?

Maybe. Maybe not.

STEP 3 – OK, they've had a bit of info about me, so now I wanted to qualify the reader and introduce an element of "realism", as a lot of profiles rush straight into doing a "me, me, me" instead of confirming to the reader why they should continue reading and thus pre-qualifying their interest. Do you pre-qualify profile visitors at the top of your profile?

Yes, if you need and want help to:

• Document your model, vision or strategy
• Save time & get results from your sales prospecting
• Require a fuller pipeline,sales funnel or CRM system
• Want increased awareness & exposure for your brand
• Grow Your Business®

STEP 4 - Next, let me explain who I help, and how I help them. You'll be amazed at how many of your competitor's profiles (in your niche or industry) simply don't say who they help, why or how. You can leverage this to your advantage. People are also fed up of people who are in love with themselves or a tad over the top, so introduce some realism (again.)

If any of the above describe your current situation then imagine a few weeks from now, experiencing the positive, permanent breakthroughs you or your stakeholders would like.

Many individuals are just too busy dealing with the symptoms of a hectic schedule and lifestyle to identify & address the root cause of their frustrations or lack of results.

Many just need a NEW plan of action.

SOME QUICK FACTS

• I have 15 books published on Amazon.
• Am author of "The Lead Generation MBA"
• I've been featured on TV - twice.
• I've over 400 testimonials on the UKs oldest social network
• I'm a former Scottish & UK Shell Livewire Winner
• Founder of Grow Your Business® Club
• For more facts, download my Keynote Speaker Kit

I WORK WITH

• Entrepreneurs
• Business Owners
• C Level Managers
• Board Members

of

• Pre start
• Start-up
• Small
• High Growth Businesses

STEP 5 –I might not be able to help them, for we need to have a chat first or at the very least they need to get in touch and tell me a bit more about how they would like me to help them. At this point, I invite them to get in touch, and they do.

I can also assist you in creating a measurable, practical plan of action via Grow Your Business® coaching or consultancy.

If required, I can also help you or your team to EXECUTE your plan.

For a FREE "Instant Breakthrough", ping me, skype me or call me on +44 1542 841319 & let's chat to see if I can help.

STEP 6 – I'm not going to bore you with the whole of my profile, but DO take a look to see how I target the reader and confirm their pain in a number of different marketing areas, and how I dangle some benefits, sizzle and case studies to help encourage them to engage with me.

Having recommendations on your profile is also a good idea.

Now let's take a look at a very powerful area of your profile -

A powerful marketing tool for your profile

The MEDIA Section on your profile
(Uploaded via Slideshare.net).

This is the section that Linkedin syncs with your Slideshare.net account and pulls in any presentations or documents you have on Slideshare or Youtube and embeds them on your Linkedin profile. To see these live examples, click the links below.

- Keynote Speaker Kit
  - https://lnkd.in/g8mnPt4
- Pipeline: Sales Prospecting System Coaching Program
  - https://lnkd.in/gpPwuJ4
- 90 Day Marketing Plan
  - https://lnkd.in/g-WQ25P
- Life Coaching
  - https://lnkd.in/ggrSr3i
- Self-Employment & Start-up Coaching
  - https://lnkd.in/gBZ8k3Y
- Thought Leadership & Becoming a Published Author
  - https://lnkd.in/gbgPiE4
- Social Media Marketing Plan
  - https://lnkd.in/gp6FdYX
- Business Development Plan
  - https://lnkd.in/gmDeKPT
- Consultancy
  - https://lnkd.in/gXW-rVy

- Catalyst Session - Situation Analysis
  - https://lnkd.in/gEj3PPz
- Lead Generation MBA Home Study Marketing Course
  - https://lnkd.in/gkXAQuQ
- Webinar Profits
  - https://lnkd.in/gtAAvPU
- Master Franchise Opportunity
  - https://lnkd.in/gS4_SYz
- FREE Instant Breakthrough
  - https://lnkd.in/ghQeUCG
- Feedback and testimonials
  - https://lnkd.in/gw3KfAs
- Books by Fraser Hay
  - https://lnkd.in/gDjcs59

The documents in the links above have been uploaded to Slideshare.net (owned by Linkedin) and then added to my profile. With the right keywords you can get your documents found on Linkedin, Slideshare, google, Bing and Yahoo.

Think of the power of that.

If you haven't already, I strongly recommend setting up a Slideshare.net account as you can get some excellent google rankings, traffic and sales by sharing your free items of value and digital assets on Slideshare.

In fact, I to help illustrate the point in the next section, and I share how I generated over 100,000 people from around the globe to a document I had on a Slideshare. Many have gone on to either download the document and then contact me or contacted me directly via my site at www.growyourbusiness.club.

ENDORSEMENTS – Now some people love them, and some people hate them. I'll let you decide what impact they could have on visitors to your profile.

99+	Online Marketing
99+	Lead Generation
99+	Social Media Marketing
99+	Email Marketing
99+	Online Advertising
99+	Marketing Strategy
84	Social Networking
99+	Entrepreneurship
62	E-commerce
70	Strategy

Do you think people will pay more attention to what you have to say if you have a lot of endorsements or none at all? Personally, I'm not sure of the real value they hold, but there is a very powerful engagement strategy on Linkedin which is all about leaving endorsements for others in your network to initiate a conversation.

In part 2, and the chapter of how to extend your network, I include some sample template emails for your to customise and use. One is a thank you to others who give you an endorsement. Use it to engage with others and to focus the conversation on how you can help them.

 Having read about the media section and endorsement sections of your profile, consider what changes or additions you might want to make to these sections.

Item of Value

OUTCOME

By the end of this stage, you will have identified what your ethical bribe, digital asset or lead magnet should be to help you build your list.

OK, so you've updated your profile to stop it reading like a CV and targeting employers to now better reflect who you are, the problems you solve, what you offer and for whom.

Now, one of the things we touched on earlier is your call to action at the end, and offering a FREE item of value. For me I offer one of 4 FREE items of value when people contact me or join my group on Linkedin. I call them an Instant Breakthrough (IBT). I offer 4 FREE IBTs, one for each stage of the Entrepreneurial Journey.

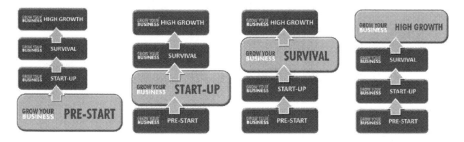

Pre-Start Entrepreneurs

If you are at a cross roads and haven't yet thought of starting a business, then download your FREE Instant Breakthrough Checklist to help you identify what's holding you back and preventing you from achieving your personal goals and objectives. Get it HERE.

Start-up Entrepreneurs

If you are struggling to document your model, vision or strategy or need help to identify why your marketing isn't working and which routes to market to focus on, then then download your FREE Instant Breakthrough Checklist to help you identify what's holding you back and preventing you from achieving your marketing goals and objectives. Get it HERE.

Existing Small Business Owners

If you're struggling to generate the results you want from your online marketing then download your FREE Instant Breakthrough Checklist to help you identify what's holding you back and preventing you from achieving your online marketing goals and objectives. Get it HERE.

High Growth Business Owners

If you're struggling to generate and record the growth you want then download your FREE Instant Breakthrough Checklist to help you identify what's holding you back and preventing you from achieving the growth you want with your business. Get it HERE.

In this example of a FREE Item of value, I created a short webinar using Youtube and simple software then uploaded it as an article on Linkedin.

It's HERE - https://www.Linkedin.com/pulse/how-generate-leads-Linkedin-fraser-hay

The more you can use different digital assets and free items of value to help educate others what it is you do and offer, the more you will be able to engage others and pull them to your profile and want to get in touch with you.

To stand out from the crowd on Linkedin, you need to position yourself as an expert. You need to decide what it is you are going to be publishing, and writing about that will help to demonstrate you are very knowledgeable and an expert within your field. You need to consider what you can give away, or promote or would like to share with your target audience that will encourage them to want to find out more about you, want to engage with you, want to buy from you or hire you.

The secret to gaining good traction, visibility and referrals online is in having **Good Quality Unique Content.** You need to create **"digital assets"** and start syndicating them on different high traffic platforms, websites and resources to help you pull visitors to your website, pre-qualify them and encourage and motivate them to want to engage with you, signup on your site or to want to request further information from you.

For example, I have over 300 videos on You Tube. I have over 100+ document uploads on Slideshare, Dokker.com and a few others, but what about you? Have you created "digital assets" for sharing your expertise online? Which of the following have you created or could you create?

- ✓ Lists
- ✓ Articles
- ✓ Photos
- ✓ Video
- ✓ Cinemagraph
- ✓ Infographics
- ✓ Interactive Infographics
- ✓ Video Infographics
- ✓ Kinetic Typography
- ✓ Graphs / Charts
- ✓ Quiz
- ✓ Poll
- ✓ Podcasts
- ✓ Image
- ✓ Animation
- ✓ Game
- ✓ Blog Posts
- ✓ Widgets / Gadgets / Badges
- ✓ Music
- ✓ Apps – Social / Mobile
- ✓ Software on CD / DVD or for download
- ✓ Books
- ✓ Ebooks
- ✓ Whitepapers / Reports
- ✓ Awards
- ✓ Contests
- ✓ Testimonials, Case Studies, Reviews or Recommendations
- ✓ Menus / Price lists, Data Sheets, Corporate "bumff"
- ✓ Press Release
- ✓ Email E-Zine or Newsletter
- ✓ Presentation
- ✓ Financial calculators

How many "digital assets" do you have? Decide what you can offer to incentivise others to want to get in contact with you, and to help you build your network of connections and your list.

Remember, once you've created your digital asset, you can upload it your Slideshare.net account, then automatically add/embed it to the media section of your Linkedin Profile.

 Make a list of "digital assets" that you could create and syndicate online or offer as a "FREE Item of value" and encourage website visitors to sign up and leave their email address in exchange for your digital asset.

Prospect Profile

OUTCOME

By the end of this stage, you will have identified specifically who your target audience is, where they congregate online & how many match your criteria.

An Ideal B2C Client Profile

If you sell to consumers and individuals, then use the following to describe what an ideal "business to consumer"(B2C) client would be to you. The more detail, the better.

Geographic

- Country, Region, County, City
- Population
- Post Code

Demographic

- Gender
- Age
- Occupation
- Marital Status
- Education
- Income
- Family size
- Home Owner

Psychographic

- Social Status/Class
- Need for status
- Role of money (does it buy material things, self-esteem, etc.?)
- Ethics/"moral compass"
- Risk-taker vs. conservative
- Spendthrift vs. hoarder of money

Sources of suspectswho match your profile.

- Facebook.com - Search
- Facebook.com – Group Search

 Use the above info to help you write down and describe what an ideal B2C customer or client would be. You can then give this profile to your advocates.

An Ideal B2B Client Profile

If you operate in the "Business to Business" arena, then use the following to describe an ideal B2B client and the criteria you want them to meet. The more detail, the better.

Geographic

*   Country, Region, County, City
*   Population
*   Post Code

Demographic

*   Industry Type (SIC)
*   Company Turnover
*   No. Employees
*   Departments
*   Head Office
*   Branch
*   Single Unit
*   SoHO
*   Year of Incorp.

Behaviour

*   What problems, issues or challenges do they have?
*   What impact is this having on their business?
*   How can you demonstrate the value of your offering?
*   How can you pre-qualify them?
*   How do you confirm that they need your help?

Sources of suspects/prospects who fit your profile.

*   Linkedin.com – Check out relevant groups
*   Facebook – Check out relevant groups

Use the above info to help you write down and describe what an ideal B2B customer or client would be. You can then give this profile to your advocates.

So, let's recap.

1. You've set your objectives and know how many sales and leads you need.
2. You've updated your profile to better qualify visitors, encouraging them to connect.
3. You've created a FREE item of value, and considered adding it to Slideshare.net.
4. Next, we want to lascr in on who we're targeting on Linkedin with your prospect profile.

So first things, first, let's use the SEARCH facility at the top of every page on Linkedin.

Here you can enter the KEYWORD of the type of person you want to target. In this example we will target all those people who are coaches (but of course you can use any keyword you want.)

There are a number of filters you can use on the right side of the page.

Connections

Your 1st tier connections are people you have already connected with, so consider reaching out to your 2nd tier connections – all those people who your tier 1 contacts are connected to.

Keywords

Here you can enter keywords to better laser in on who exactly it is you want to reach, and here you can enter their Firstname, Surname, Title, Company or the school they attended.

Location

Here you can select the country, county or city that you wish to target. This can be very useful if you are doing a local campaign or inviting people to a local event.

Current Companies

Here you can add companies you wish to target that people are currently working at or in.

Past Companies

Here you can add companies you wish to target that people have previously at or in.

Profile Language

Here you can select which language you wish to target. Current options include English, French, Spanish, Dutch and Portugese.

Non Profit Interests

Here you can select whether they volunteer for a non-profit or charitable organisation or serve on their board.

Create a search alert

Here you can save your search criteria, and get an alert everytime a new member profile matches your criteria.

There are many more criteria you can use when you upgrade your account.

Imagine if you could automate your targeting and message sending to prospective contacts who match your criteria. What impact could that have to your prospecting and conversions?

 Now grab a pen and paper and make a list of the criteria you want your prospects to match before using the people search to find them.

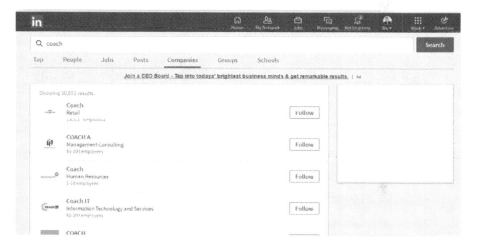

You can also use the company search facility to help you target prospective customers.

Another aspect of your prospective client profile to consider is the communities or groups they congregate or contribute in, online. By entering your keyword and selecting groups, in the quick example above, you can see that from joining the first 5 results above, you could potentially reach over 200,000 peoples who are members of those coaching groups on Linkedin.

Now, a little known useful tool is the Linkedin Share App which we will explain more about in the next chapter when you extend your network.

.

Extend Your Network

OUTCOME

By the end of this stage, you will have Identified different practical, proven & powerful tactics to extend your network, fill your pipeline, funnel & CRM system.

So, let's recap.

1. You've set your objectives and know how many sales and leads you need.
2. You've updated your profile to better qualify visitors, encouraging them to connect.
3. You've created a FREE item of value, and considered adding it to Slideshare.net.
4. You've created a prospect profile so you know who you are targeting on Linkedin.
5. Now it's time to extend your network.

Viewing other people's profiles

So obvious, but many people don't realise the power of this. It can be very effective. Simply enter your keyword into people search, and to view the person's profile, simply click on their name. Why do this? For Linkedin will automatically email the person, telling them that you have viewed their profile.

Their natural curiosity and your perfectly honed profile headline will encourage them to want to view yours and if you followed the hints and tips shared earlier, they will want to connect with you and request your free item of value / digital asset.

Two important things to say at this point:

Remember

1. Linkedin is emailing them NOT you
2. If your headline is well crafted, they will choose to visit your profile

Think of the power of that and the massive amounts of time it will save you.

Group Members

You can do a variation on a theme here, by doing a group search, signing into a particular group and then clicking on the profiles of the group members for better targeting.

After all, the members of that group are interested in that particular topic of subject, and if you've done your homework, you could pull hundreds of members from that group to your profile in a single day.

Remember, there's no email to send them, you're simply targeting them & clicking their profile.

If you want to send them an email, I share a number of template emails later in the book.

Remember the share app from last chapter?

If you click on **"post to groups"**, when you share an article or any url, you can share it in multiple groups simultaneously reaching hundreds of thousands of potential prospects.

The url and format to use is -
https://www.Linkedin.com/cws/share?url=http://www.url.com
Simply change http://www.url.com to the url of the post, webpage or website you want to share.

Write an article

Write an article via your home page status bar and when you publish it, ensure you select public and twitter, to help get maximum exposure.

Now, If you're struggling what to decide to write about then here's 50 ideas for blogging and writing articles, then using just one suggestion per week from the list below, you have a year-long blogging and article writing strategy to integrate an share in your prospecting online –

1. Who's done an excellent job for you - write a positive case study for them.
2. Customer CASE STUDIES - Remind readers of your successes
3. Common MISTAKES that people make, and how to avoid them
4. Daily Topical News
5. Share some interesting FACTS about your INDUSTRY
6. A relevant HUMOUROUS story to show you have a sense of humour
7. Who has really p****d you off or let you down. Share your experience.
8. Search YOUTUBE relevant topics and embed videos into your blog
9. Create your own VIDEOS and embed them into your blog
10. Embed your own POWERPOINTS from Slideshare.net into your blog
11. Debunk a Myth about your industry

12. Write about something you're PASSIONATE about

13. Embed your own .PDF documents from docstoc.com into your blog

14. Customer PAIN - Remind your readers of the problems you solve

15. Embed your own WORD documents from scribd.com into your blog

16. Share some interesting FACTS about your PRODUCTS & SERVICES

17. Share the PROBLEMS of your INDUSTRY and some potential SOLUTIONS

18. Do you have some amazing facts that you want to share with visitors?

19. Invite GUEST BLOGGERS to post relevant content into your blog

20. Is there a CAUSE or CHARITY that you care about?

21. Create a top 10 TIPS outlining some hints and tips for blog readers

22. Include a wee poll or survey in your blog

23. Share your views of the WORLD

24. Write a list of FAQs of potential objections for your services & address each one

25. Ask a question in your headline to draw people into your blog

26. Use Pingler.com or Bulkping.com to "Ping" your blog url

27. Industry TRENDS - What are the emerging markets/opportunities?

28. Include your own infographics in your blogs

29. Explain how a particular PROCESS works - Break it down for people

30. Debunk a Myth about your products and services

31. Is there a local CAUSE or COMMUNITY project that you feel strongly about?

32. If you don't have any goto google images & search for "keyword infographic"

33. Industry NEWS - What's happening in your Niche?

34. Do a software walk thru using screengrabs in your blogs using capturewizpro

35. Include a screengrab of a product in a product review

36. Share the FRUSTRATIONS of your INDUSTRY

37. Whose book have you read lately? Write a review

38. Who has really p****d you off or let you down. Share your experience.

39. Do you have some excellent market research findings you want to share?

40. Have someone interview you, and record it?

41. Why not interview someone else and record it?

42. Share an experience about a RISK you took, and the REWARD you got

43. Ask for OPINIONS on a particular topic or Issue

44. Debunk a Myth about you

45. Share some interesting FACTS about YOU

46. Share a solution to a specific, RELEVANT problem

47. Embed a PHOTO from Flickr or Photobucket (funny, strange, topical etc)

48. Embed a VIDEO testimonial

49. Write an upbeat INSPIRATIONAL post to give your readers a mental boost

50. AUDIO Record your Blog and upload to iTUNES (or similar.)

Whatever you decide, Remember:

An article could be a SPEAKING TOPIC for your speaking engagements

An article could be converted into a PODCAST

An article could be converted into a VIDEO

An article could be converted into a WEBINAR

An article could be converted into a POWERPOINT

An article could be converted into a PDF Document

2-3 articles could be a chapter in your next BOOK

5 or 7 articles could be an EMAIL COURSE

10 articles or more could be an EBOOK or KINDLE BOOK

Now, once you've written your article you could of course use the sharing app to promote it in each of your targeted groups. Remember by posting the article to PUBLIC, and by sharing in the groups that you are a member of – will attract new people to you. You want to be seen as an expert and sharing useful information with your target audience.

One article, I've written on Linkedin has had over 250,000 views, over 500 likes and over 150 comments. It's HERE.

Pingler.com

Another useful tool is Pingler.com which enables you to promote articles, status updates, group posts out to the wider internet to maximise exposure for your post. You simply enter the url and keyword, select a category, it then "pings" your url to a number of online services, databases, search engines & directories.

Don't forget Slideshare.net

When you add a presentation or document to Slideshare.net you can then copy the url and share it in a public status update on Linkedin. There are 3 benefits to this:

1. Your Slideshare document will get views in Slideshare and Linkedin
2. With good keywords in your title, description & tags you'll get excellent google juice

3. You can select "Add to profile" in your "Uploads Section" on Slideshare to add the file automatically to the Media Section of your profile on Linkedin too.

This can be an excellent magnet for pulling people to you.

One document I have on Slideshare has generated over 100,000 views from across the globe.

Ask for Introductions

Sometimes we can see that people in our network are connected to people who meet the criteria in our prospect profile. It often pays to ask for an introduction. More often than not, it can result in a skype conversation, an appointment and even a sale. Later in the book, I share an example email you may wish to consider using.

Import names into your network

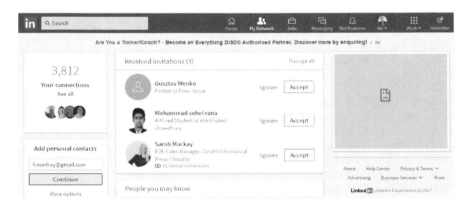

This is a simple 3 step process.

1. Click the "My Network" icon at the top of the page on Linkedin.
2. **Click on "Continue"**

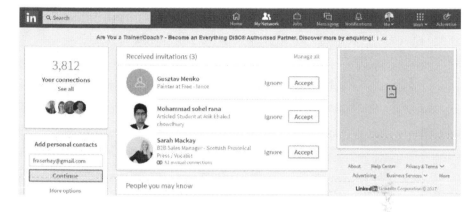

Click on "More Options" and you are ready for Linkedin to import people from your email address book on various platforms such as gmail, yahoo, outlook or aol.

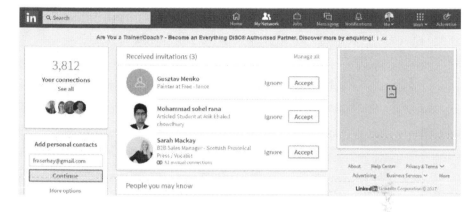

Contributing in Groups

We've already mentioned using groups to target communities of potential prospects and that the search facility in Linkedin can help you confirm which groups your prospects have joined.

When you have done your research and joined a group, ensure you contribute, by liking, and commenting other member's posts. As mentioned earlier, people are naturally curious as to who is liking and commenting on their posts, and they will visit your profile.

If you've updated your profile, then there's a good chance they will want to join your network and engage with you.

Remember your prospecting mantra as it's so true when prospecting via groups on Linkedin –

"Giver's gain, takers drain and lurkers simply remain the same."

The more you contribute and help others, the more visible you are and the more people will recognise that you are knowledgeable and helpful and will want to engage with you.

Lead, don't follow

OUTCOME

By the end of this stage, you will have identified powerful tactics to position you as a thought leader & expert in your niche, sector or marketplace.

An excellent way to help build your list and fill your pipeline is to create your own group. Think about it. Imaging having a community online where people want to go and contribute knowing they will get your help, guidance and support.

A group should be treated like a bank account.

The more you contribute, the more the value increases, the more visible and respected you become.

The more the members contribute to it, the more the value further increases.

If people just take from the group, guess what? The value decreases.

Once again, our prospecting mantra comes into play –

"Givers gain, takers drain and lurkers simply remain the same."

Some groups on Linkedin have over 250,000 members. Imaging if you had a list that big.

At the time of writing, my own group is small, it's tight and it's brand new, but I wanted to explain why I set it up, and how I'm promoting it. As a thank you for joining it, I'd like to say thank you by offering 2 things –

1. A Free Instant Breakthrough (as previously mentioned)
2. A personal chat to discuss mutual opportunities and how we can help each other.

NOW CLAIM YOUR FREE

INSTANT BREAKTHROUGH

Yes, I want my FREE **INSTANT BREAKTHROUGH**

https://www.Linkedin.com/groups/13517487

There's a couple of interesting features about setting up your own group, and I'll share them here. There's a few things you should do, that can save you a great deal of time and energy and better assist potential members too.

* I acknowledge and agree that the logo/image I am uploading does not infringe upon any third party copyrights, trademarks, or other proprietary rights or otherwise violate the User Agreement.

* Group Name:

Note: "LinkedIn" is not allowed to be used in your group name

* Summary: Enter a brief description about your group and its purpose. Your summary about this group will appear in the Groups Directory.

* Description: Your full description of this group will appear on your group pages

Website:

When you create your group, give it a name, brief summary, description and add the url of your own website. Also give thought to the type of group you want.

Standard Group

Any member can invite other members and the group will appear in the search results

Unlisted

The group admin only can invite new members, and it won't appear in the search results.

I also recommend setting up a rules page, so that members know what the etiquette is for the group and what may be expected of them (or not) as the case may be. A little tip I would suggest for this page, is perhaps call it your "rules & tools" page where you share some elementary hints, tips, tools and resources to help your new members too. It helps to reinforce a positive message and the ethos of your group – which should be all about helping and sharing with your members whilst encouraging them to do the same. (Remember your new prospecting mantra ;))

Templates

There is also a feature to set up a number of different template emails to be sent manually or automatically depending on your preferences. You can set up messages for the following actions:

1. **Request-to-join:** A reply to be sent to all requests to join
2. **Welcome Message:** Thank them and tell them what to do inside the group
3. **Decline Message:** If you don't want them to become a member
4. **Decline-and-Block Message:** Send this if for "awkward" & persistent offenders.

Send Invitations

This is straight forward. You add the connections from your network that you would like to invite to join, then click "Send Invitations" and Linkedin does the rest. It's got an informal tone to it as they are already in your network.

In the next chapter, we'll share some emails that you may wish to consider using for invitations to chat, join your network and group.

Send an Announcement

This is a very useful feature, as it enables you to send a message to all the members of your group. This is an excellent way to stay in touch with your members or to profile a particular member, service or special offer that your members could benefit from.

Remember Pingler.com?

Don't forget to Pingler your group url to help get the home page spidered & indexed outside of Linkedin to help increase the exposure and awareness of who you are and what you offer.

Position yourself as a thought leader

I have a saying – "Everyone has a book in them" and it's true. Think of all the knowledge, wisdom and experience you have amassed over the years, the stories you could tell, and the hints, tips and know how you have to solve problems and perform certain tasks. I've written and published 15 books on Amazon and speak on a number of different topics too.

My author page is <u>HERE</u>.

I've also created a coaching program on how to publish your own book and generate downloads.

My digital Profits coaching program overview is <u>HERE</u>.

Invite to chat

OUTCOME

By the end of this stage, you will have added new names to your funnel, pipeline & CRM system, ready to move them to the next stage of your sales process .

You've probably received an email on Linkedin, and thought – "Spam".

Or, you've seen that you got an email from someone you don't know and did not respond to it.

The emails (and headlines) offered as templates by Linkedin can be a little impersonal and ineffective. In this chapter, I want to share a few template emails for you to consider using personalizing and customizing for your own prospecting and engagement on Linkedin.

A simple and powerful "signature" to your emails is to say that you are the founder or owner of a group on Linkedin. This will help to position you as a leader, and not just another follower.

You may want to have your own collection of rapid response emails stored in a simple text file, so you can cut n paste them into your messaging centre on Linkedin when you want to send them. The secret is to make them conversational in nature and wanting to build the relationship.

Far too many people fail by sending proposals or asking for a sale in the first communication.

EMAIL #1 - Following up people who've viewed your profile

Hi <name>

Thanks for taking a peek at my profile. Is there anything in particular I can help with?

In case you didn't know, I've also recently set up a NEW group on Linkedin, that could be of mutual benefit to us both. (It's brand new.)

https://www.Linkedin.com/groups/13517487

As we grow, I think members may benefit from what you do and offer. See you inside.

It's early days, but we don't know just how big it could get.

Kind Regards

Fraser
Founder | Grow Your Business® Network

EMAIL #2 - Accepting Contact Requests

Hi

I've accepted your contact request. We're now connected. Is there anything in particular I can help with?

If you're wanting to raise your profile and build good solid connections here on Linkedin, can I recommend you also joining my new group.

I suspect there will be excellent mutual benefit to us both in the fullest of time. (It's brand new.)

https://www.Linkedin.com/groups/13517487

As we grow, I think members may benefit from what you do and offer. See you inside.

It's early days, but we don't know just how big it could get.

Kind Regards

Fraser
Founder | Grow Your Business® Network

EMAIL #3 - New Connections Accepting Your Invite

Hi

Thanks for connecting. Is there anything in particular I can help with?

Take a look at my profile, and in particular, the media section to see what I'm up to.

I also recommend you also join my new group.

I suspect there will be excellent mutual benefit to us both in the fullest of time. (It's brand new.)

https://www.Linkedin.com/groups/13517487

As we grow, I think members may benefit from what you do and offer. See you inside.

It's early days, but we don't know just how big it could get.

And please, if I can help in any way, just ask ;)

Kind Regards

Fraser
Founder | Grow Your Business® Network

EMAIL #4 - Contacting Members of other Groups
(having viewed their profile)

Hi <name>

We're both members of [GROUP NAME], and thought it would be good to be connected.

Shall we?

Kind Regards

Fraser
Founder | Grow Your Business® Network

EMAIL #5 - Contacting Members of other Groups – Version 2

Hi <name>

We're both members of [GROUP NAME], and thought it would be good to be connected.

I'm founder of the Group Your Business Group Here on Linkedin. Maybe we can both benefit from being connected.

Shall we?

Kind Regards

Fraser
Founder | Grow Your Business® Network

EMAIL #6 - Contacting Group Member
(having contributed to their post)

Hi <name>

I really enjoyed your post in the [NAME] group.

[LINK TO POST]

I would like to connect and stay in touch with what you're up to.

Shall we?

Kind Regards

Fraser
Founder | Grow Your Business® Network

EMAIL #7 - Contacting Members you've found via search

Hi <name>

I stumbled across your profile and wondered if you would like to connect?

Shall we?

Kind Regards

Fraser
Founder | Grow Your Business® Network

EMAIL #8 - Contacting Members you've found via search – version 2

Hi <name>

I stumbled across your profile and wondered if you would like to connect?

I'm founder of the Group Your Business Group here on Linkedin. Maybe we can both benefit from being connected.

Shall we?

Kind Regards

Fraser
Founder | Grow Your Business® Network

EMAIL #9 – Alternate thanks for the connection

Hi <name>

Many thanks adding me to your network.

I'm a little stacked up next few days, but I will contact you at the beginning of next week to arrange a convenient time to chat so we can get to know each other better and I can find out more about what you offer.

Kind Regards

Fraser
Founder | Grow Your Business® Network

EMAIL #10 – Follow-up to #9

Hi <name>

Last week we connected on Linkedin and I told you I would follow up with you.

Like I said before I wanted to have a quick chat with you about your business and what sets you apart from your competitors.

Drop me a line when is convenient to chat by phone or skype.

Regards

Fraser
Skype: Pocketmentor. Tel: +44(0)1542841319
www.fraserhay.co.uk

EMAIL #11 – Ask permission to send your Free Item of value

Hi <name>

Thanks for the connection, I have something that may be of interest that I'd like to share with you as a thank you for connecting.

Drop me a quick line to confirm whether you'd like me to send it you or not.

Thanks

Regards

Fraser
Skype: Pocketmentor. Tel: +44(0)1542841319
www.fraserhay.co.uk

EMAIL #12 – After someone thanks you for liking or commenting on their post

Hi <name>

No Problem. I really enjoyed it.
I'd also welcome the opportunity to stay in touch to see what else you're up to.

Let's connect.

Thanks

Regards

Fraser
Skype: Pocketmentor. Tel: +44(0)1542841319
www.fraserhay.co.uk

Nurturing the relationship

OUTCOME

By the end of this stage, you will be filling your sales funnel, hosting skype chats, securing appointments, winning clients, closing business & new deals .

After you've been connected, you'd probably want to stay in touch. There's a good systematic approach to take in order to achieve this. It's all about being prepared and it's also about being personable and taking an active interest in your connections.

After you've connected with them, leave it a few days or so, then consider sending the following emails in sequence. You can also change them around or use emails from the last chapter.

The secret is obvious – it's to build on the relationship you've started.

EMAIL #13 – Message Sequence #1

Hi <name>

I just published this article and would love your thoughts and opinion of it.

[ARTICLE URL ON LINKEDIN]

We've overdue for a catch-up too.

Regards

Fraser
Skype: Pocketmentor. Tel: +44(0)1542841319
www.fraserhay.co.uk

EMAIL #14 – Message Sequence #2

Hi <name>

Have you seen this group discussion in [GROUP]?

I'd be interested in your thoughts and comments.

[GROUP POST URL]

Hope all is well.

Regards

Fraser
Skype: Pocketmentor. Tel: +44(0)1542841319
www.fraserhay.co.uk

EMAIL #15 – Message Sequence - #3

Hi <name>

We've been connected on here for a wee while now But we still haven't had a chance to catch up by Phone or skype yet to discuss how we might be able to help each other.

Are you free Tuesday or Wednesday next week for a chat? No pitch. No agenda. Just a natter.

Regards

Fraser
Skype: Pocketmentor. Tel: +44(0)1542841319
www.fraserhay.co.uk

EMAIL #16 – Message Sequence - #4

Hi <name>

Just following to organise having a chat if you're up For it. Ping to arrange a convenient time to chat.

Regards

Fraser
Skype: Pocketmentor. Tel: +44(0)1542841319
www.fraserhay.co.uk

EMAIL #17 – Common connection

Hi <name>

I see we're connected to [INDIVIDUAL] and wondered if you'd like to connect too.
Thanks

Fraser
Founder | Grow Your Business® Network

EMAIL #18 – Asking for an introduction

Hi <name>

We've been connected on here for a while now and I see you're connected to [INDIVIDUAL] .

Would it be possible to get an introduction to them As I'd love to have a chat with them.

Thanks

Fraser
Founder | Grow Your Business® Network

EMAIL #19 – Thanking someone for an endorsement

Hi <name>

Just a quickie to say thanks for endorsing my [SKILLS] skills.
As a thank you, I'd like to invite you to join my group because I think some of my members could benefit from your skills.

https://www.Linkedin.com/groups/13517487

As we grow, I think more and more members may benefit from what you do and offer. See you inside.

It's early days, but we don't know just how big it could get.

Kind Regards

Fraser
Founder | Grow Your Business® Network

EMAIL #20 – When someone thanks you for endorsing them

Hi <name>

No problem.

I'd like to invite you to join my group because I think some of my members could also benefit from your skills.

https://www.Linkedin.com/groups/13517487

As we grow, I think more and more members may benefit From what you do and offer. See you inside.

It's early days, but we don't know just how big it could get.

Kind Regards

Fraser
Founder | Grow Your Business® Network

EMAIL #21 – Lost touch and re-connecting

Hi <name>

I was browsing through my contacts, and noticed
We hadn't been in touch with each other a while.

I'd love to organise a chat by skype or phone to Hear about what you've been up to.

When's good for you?

Kind Regards

Fraser
Founder | Grow Your Business® Network

Exceed your expectations

OUTCOME

By the end of this stage, you will be able to prove to yourself that its working with real time reporting & daily emails to confirm your progress & results.

Managing expectation can sometimes be difficult. It can be more difficult if you don't have a plan or a system to follow on a daily basis. Here, I've enclosed a daily activity sheet to help you stay focused as you work towards building relationships and filling your pipeline.

Access your daily activity sheet on Slideshare – HERE.

It's very easy to go onto Linkedin, and before you know it you've read updates, looked at emails, gone to groups, view other people's posts and a couple of hours have passed and you have nothing to show for it.

It pays to plan.

Using your daily activity worksheet, the first thing you need to do is set your daily goals for 5 specific outcomes:

Connections

This is how many new connections you want to achieve today. Consider visiting people's profiles, asking for connections with fellow group members and people in your area.

Conversations

This is how many of those new connections you want to engage with. Think about thanking people for liking and commenting on your updates, images, articles, Slideshare documents and your group posts.

Appointments

How many appointments are you aiming to get? How many emails will you send using the templates from the last chapter? You know what to do, so just do it.

Sales

How many sales are you hoping to achieve today? If you completed the exercise in setting your sales objectives you'll know exactly how much you need to make. I'm sure your boss or life partner will keep you posted on that front too ;)

Endorsements/Referrals

How many are you aiming to receive today? More importantly, how many will you give? You know what to do, and how to thank people as well as how to continue the conversation.

Your Priority Goal for the day

Here you want to write down what it is you want to achieve by the end of the day.

How you spend your time

Now, how you spend your time is entirely up to you, but a good idea is to write down which elements of your prospecting, marketing and selling you will do in the day ahead. It might be 5 things you do at different times of the day, it might just be 1 – 2 hours focusing on a very specific aspect of your prospecting – you decide how you will spend your day.

A reminder of what to do is on the right side of the page.

You can always return and read the book too, or learn advanced tactics in the coaching program.

Record the challenges, lessons and success you've encountered.

This is good to help you summarise what you've achieved or what you specifically need help with in order to experience the breakthroughs you want.

Now here are 10 common mistakes you will want to avoid with your prospecting online. It will serve as a refresher & reminder of what not to do with everything we've covered up until now.

Ready? Let's begin…

Mistake #1 – Not focusing on your prospects.

Don't make the classic mistake of not stating who you work with and who you can help. Ensure you list the types of people you can assist and the problems, needs or frustrations that they may suffer from. This helps to qualify people.

Update your profile to apply the key point above.

Mistake #2 – Not getting found on search results

Ensure you have your keyword or phrase in your name, headline, position fields, summary & "specialties". Also ensure you select the correct "category". Review often.

 Update your profile to apply the key point above.

Mistake #3 – Having a boring headline

"Manager at xyz Ltd." Or "Marketing Coach & Author of the Lead Generation MBA: 2500 Ways to generate leads, sales and referrals". Give them a reason to want to click your profile. Remember your headline is included in all discussion posts.

 Update your profile to apply the key point above.

Mistake #4 – Forgetting to add your telephone number

Believe me it does happen. You may also want to tell visitors of your profile what to do next. Here's an example: Before choosing to contact me by phone, by Skype or by email via my profile, please do the following:

1. Read my profile here on Linkedin, and view the entire Slideshare presentation
2. Sign up for my FREE marketing audit at my website.

Then if you have any questions, comments or are interested in my marketing coaching services, then please feel free to contact me. I also welcome teleseminar, webinar, keynote and event speaking opportunities as well JV opportunities. Please do get in touch.

 Update your profile to apply the key point above.

Mistake #5 – Not asking for recommendations

Testimonials and recommendations help sell you and your services. Period.

 Update your profile to apply the key point above.

Mistake #6 – Not completing your profile

Have you won any awards? Have you added the Slideshare application to your profile yet? Go on complete your profile.

 Update your profile to apply the key point above.

Mistake #7– Not participating in relevant groups

Do you want to sign up for groups with thousands of your competitors, or do you want to join groups containing members who NEED your services. Whatever you decide, ensure you participate and get seen in these groups.

Things you can do in groups are:
- Start a controversial discussion
- Like other people's posts
- Answer people's questions.
- Write a thought provoking posts

 You can join 50 groups on Linkedin. Ensure you join 50 groups.

Mistake #8 – Waiting for people to contact you

Update your status at least daily. Use your status to point to your latest ads, offers and posts on your own blog.

 Update your profile to apply the key point above.

Mistake #9 – Not starting your own group

Makes sense really, doesn't it. Don't just spend time in other people's groups, build your own community and entice people to come to yours with good relevant, helpful content. Ensure you encourage members to share, and that they follow your rules. Don't expect them just to join because you've set it up. Give them a reason – a free gift such as a report or free consultation to encourage them to want to join your group.

 Update your profile to apply the key point above.

Mistake #10 – Failing to Build Your List

Whether it's via your status activity, participating in other groups, ads or via emails sent to your own group list, you want to get people signing up to the squeeze page on your own website for your Free Item of Value. Also don't forget to personalise your Linkedin profile url via "settings".

 Update your profile to apply the key point above.

Motivate & enthuse yourself to make it happen

Probably one of the most important factors in social networking is tenacity and a personal commitment to your business. That's why a daily routine is important.

The hardest part of any business is to generate leads and enquiries, but you'd be amazed by the number of people who fail to **follow up** a new network contact – be they a fan, follower, friend or prospect simply because they said "**NO**" the first time they were asked.

Or that they simply didn't get in touch, despite that their contact details were logged on your profile hits page.

Follow up the last 4 people who visited your Linkedin profile. Thank them for visiting and ask them how you can help them. Go on, do it now.

Your ability to follow up prospects and enquiries is pivotal to your success in ANY business, and as a professional networker on Linkedin.com. The secret to succeeding in networking is to engage other people and motivate them to action, **always thinking of them first and yourself second.**

As Steven Covey puts it – "Seek first to understand, then to be understood."

In short, you must follow up, follow up, follow up.

Remember, there are a number of different ways, and combinations of different ways that you can communicate with your network.

Email
Status Update
Group posts
Telephone
Skype
Google hangouts & live webinars
Ezine / Newsletter

 What is your contact schedule for communicating with your network? How often do you follow up and communicate with your network sharing links and content from your site?

The objective of following up prospects is to get them to respond and enter into dialogue and a conversation with you either via Linkedin, phone, email, instant messenger/SKYPE, personal or direct message via the platform or in person via a 121 or appointment.

Once you are in dialogue with them, and gain rapport, you can then focus on building a relationship by being selfless and focusing your attention on your network contact and how you can help them...

PLEASE NOTE: It's not uncommon, for it to take 3, 4 or more follow-ups on Linkedin.com, to get the desired result. So find a reason to stay in touch, update or share something with your connections. It will pay great dividends in the future.

If you're succeeding with your prospecting, but need help in closing deals and winning clients then you may want to take a closer look at our sales coaching program.

Part Three – Widening your net

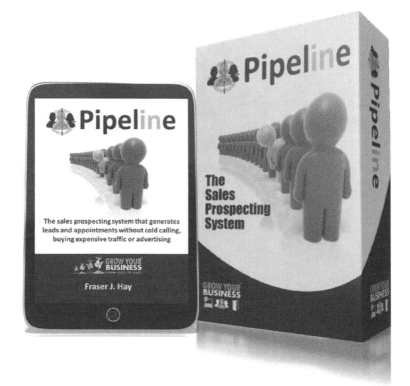

Achieving even greater results

Getting Found on Slideshare and the search engines

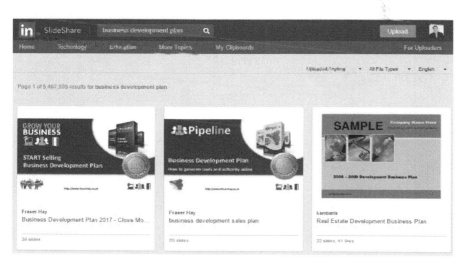

As mentioned, previously, I've added a number of presentations to Slideshare.net. By making sure that your Title, Description and Tags contain targeted keywords, you can get your content to rank high in the search results. The example above beat 5.4m for the #1 position on Slideshare.

You can then add the presentation to your Linkedin Profile, and using some of the tools mentioned earlier such as twitter, Facebook, Google Plus and Pingler, you can also generate backlinks and traffic to your new digital asset or embed it into your articles and blog posts. The more you share your digital asset, the greater the likelihood of getting high rankings in the top 3 search engines too.

Here's another example –

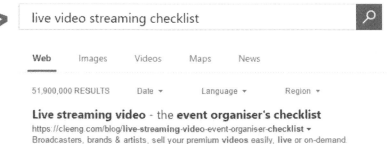

That document on Slideshare beat over 50m other results for a page 1 ranking and it got ranked on page 1 of yahoo as well. Now with a bit of careful research, and selecting good keywords when adding presentations and documents to Slideshare, think what you could achieve.

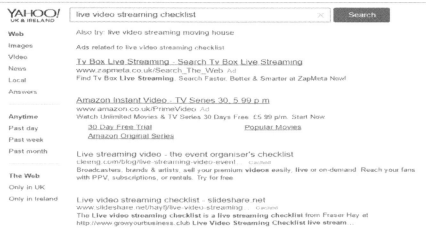

Another interesting thing you can do on Slideshare is to embed a youtube video into your presentation to get it found on Slideshare and the external search engines too.

Remember the webinar I shared earlier in the book? Well I embedded the video from Youtube into a different presentation uploaded to Slideshare.

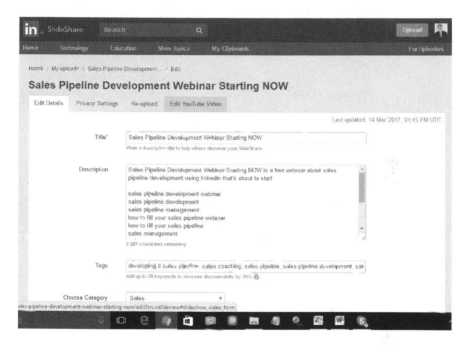

Once saved, the video gets placed into the first slide of the presentation.

I then shared it on Linkedin, Google Plus, Facebook, Twitter and Pingler.com.

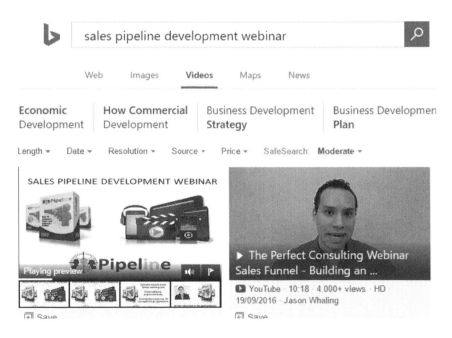

Voila! It came up #1 in the video search results on Bing.com

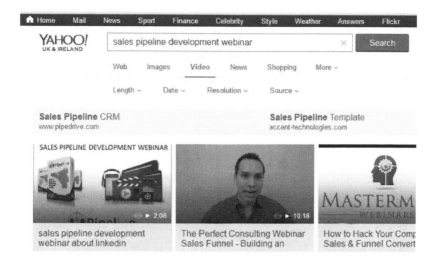

It also came up #1 in the video search results on Yahoo.com.

You have test, test, test.

Test your headlines, descriptions keywords and tags.

Test different approaches, and calls to action.

Test video, test embedding video in your presentations, articles and blogs.

You might just be surprised at what you can achieve across different platforms.

Combine the different approaches above for even more exposure. What about the video search results on Google?

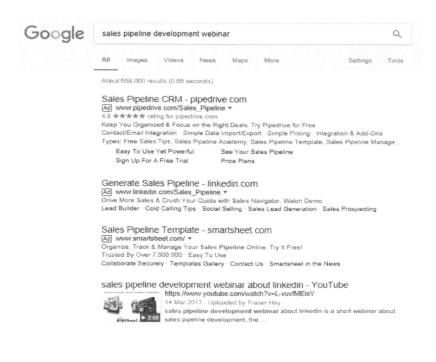

Google | sales pipeline development webinar

All   Images   Videos   News   Maps   More   Settings   Tools

About 18,700 results (0.36 seconds)

sales pipeline development webinar about linkedin - YouTube
https://www.youtube.com/watch?v=L-vuvfMEisY
14 Mar 2017 - Uploaded by Fraser Hay
sales pipeline development webinar about linkedin is a short webinar about sales pipeline development, the ...

UnLtd Webinar: Creating Opportunities Developing your sales ...
https://www.youtube.com/watch?v=I8pk9MhUQ5I ▾
11 Nov 2014 - Uploaded by UnLtd For Social Entrepreneurs
UnLtd **Webinar**: Creating Opportunities **Developing** your **sales pipeline** and sales techniques. UnLtd For ...

Stimulating Sales in an Uncertain Climate: The Role of Branding and ...
www.sciencemag.org/.../webinars/stimulating-sales-uncertain-climat...
Currently, the role of marketing departments is largely seen as **sales** support. ... This **webinar** is brought to ...

How to Generate Leads on Linkedin - Webinar NOW - YouTube
https://www.youtube.com/watch?v=FSXOKE7wF0Y
14 Mar 2017 - Uploaded by Fraser Hay
how to generate leads on linkedin is a short **webinar** starting now about ... how to fill your **sales pipeline** ...

Even on the generic search results on Google too.

Google | sales pipeline development webinar

All   Images   Videos   News   Maps   More   Settings   Tools

About 558,000 results (0.65 seconds)

Sales Pipeline CRM - pipedrive.com
[Ad] www.pipedrive.com/Sales_Pipeline ▾
4.8 ★★★★★ rating for pipedrive.com
Keep You Organised & Focus on the Right Deals. Try Pipedrive for Free
Contact/Email Integration · Simple Data Import/Export · Simple Pricing · Integration & Add-Ons
Types: Free Sales Tips, Sales Pipeline Academy, Sales Pipeline Template, Sales Pipeline Manage...
Easy To Use Yet Powerful   See Your Sales Pipeline
Sign Up For A Free Trial   Price Plans

Generate Sales Pipeline - linkedin.com
[Ad] www.linkedin.com/Sales_Pipeline ▾
Drive More Sales & Crush Your Quota with Sales Navigator. Watch Demo.
Lead Builder · Cold Calling Tips · Social Selling · Sales Lead Generation · Sales Prospecting

Sales Pipeline Template - smartsheet.com
[Ad] www.smartsheet.com/ ▾
Organize, Track & Manage Your Sales Pipeline Online. Try It Free!
Trusted By Over 7,000,000 · Easy To Use
Collaborate Securely · Templates Gallery · Contact Us · Smartsheet in the News

sales pipeline development webinar about linkedin - YouTube
https://www.youtube.com/watch?v=L-vuvfMEisY
14 Mar 2017 - Uploaded by Fraser Hay
sales pipeline development webinar about linkedin is a short webinar about sales pipeline development, the ...

110

Getting Found on Linkedin

So do you want to know how I achieved those results? Right then, here you go...

1. Ensure your "**Professional Headline**" stands out. This is area right next to your photo at the top of your profile. I try to pull people into my profile, by offering a FREE "Instant breakthrough or chat". What will you offer?

2. Ensure your "**Current Position**" contains the keywords by which you want to be found. Ideally, you want your Keyword(s) at least 3 times in here.

3. Ensure your "**Past**" work position(s) contains the keywords by which you want to be found. Ideally, you want your Keyword(s) at least once in here.

4. Ensure the "**Summary**" Area" of your profile contains the keywords by which you want to be found. Ideally, at least once.

5. Ensure the "**Specialties**" Area of your profile contains the keywords by which you want to be found. Again, ideally at least once.

6. Ensure you fill out your profile as completely possible.

7. Offer a **FREE ITEM** of **VALUE** (such as a free report, video or consultation, this will help to draw people in and build your list.

8. Offer to write a recommendation for those you've done business with.

9. When completing your **Summary Section**, refer back to **earlier in the book** for tips on how to engage prospects and visitors to your profile. Ensure your summary section both educates and qualifies your reader. Remember, prospects are silently begging to be led, so guide them through your engagement process.

10. By Listing the relevant "**Skills**" on your profile, will also help recruiters and those who are seeking contractors and consultants to find you quicker.

 Make the relevant changes to your profile to help you get found on Linkedin's search results and start increasing your profile views and enquiries.

Your Professional Headline Builder

Simply answer each of the questions below, and then join some or all of your answers together to create a headline for your profile. You can then amend to suit.

What benefit will you product or Service offer the customer (or what pain will it alleviate)? In other words, what is the general benefit that you offer. E.g. Save money, 100% uptime, lose weight, stay focused, save energy, and make more money.	A
To whom do you provide this to? (Your Target Audience) e.g. Do you know the Geographic, Demographic, Psychographic or Corporate Profile of your clients?	B
How quickly can you help your customer accomplish this goal? When stating your answer, ensure you include both the number and the timeframe. e.g. 60 minutes, 24 hours, 7 days, 4 weeks,12months etc.	C
What are the results a customer can expect upon reaching this goal? Please specify and quantify the type of results and the amount/value. e.g. save £1000, make £5000, lose 8 lbs., earn 7%, pay only 2%	D

How many steps, secrets, tips or methods are you giving the customer in order to achieve the results? Please specify and quantify the type of results and the amount/value. e.g. 7 secrets, 3 simple steps, 6 x 30 minute sessions, 5 unique Ways, Over 50 hints & tips	E
What is the first Qualifying Question you ask your prospective clients? Please write down the exact question. e.g. Struggling to generate leads? Are you wrestling with social media?	

 Use the profile headline builder to create 4 new headlines for your profile.

Please note Your Killer Qualifying Question can be used in your profile Summary to help qualify the person reading your profile. Or it could be used in blogs or group posts.

Want some other template examples? OK, Here you go:-

Below is a list of fill-in-the-blanks template headlines that are ready to use.

Discover How This [Job Title] Helps [Target Audience] [Benefit1] by [Results]

~

Client Admits [Problem] Because of [Cause]. How much is your [problem] really costing you?
Contact me Now.

~

Discover why companies like [Famous Brand 1], [famous Brand 2], and [Famous Brand3]
have hired me to help with their [Job function]
0
~

Do you require someone to manage your [Project] project and complete on time, within budget,
and to your exact requirements?

~

Do you recognise the [X] early warning signs of [problem] and what to do about it?

~

[Job Title] Specialises in Helping Companies & Global organisations Avoid [Common Problem] costing upwards of [Big Bucks]
~

Discover A [Job Title] who achieved [Results] in less than [timescale]

~

Client Admits Losing £10m Because of Poor Marketing. How Much Is Your Marketing Really Costing You? Find out for FREE.

~

10 Things every [Job Title] should know about [Topic], but don't mention it in their CV

~

[XX%] of [Job Title] within the [industry] Industry often fail to address [Number] common issues, challenges & obstacles.

~

I generated [Results] for [Client/Employer] and would like to do the same for you too.

~

"[Results based testimonial.]"

~

Do you Need to [Benefit 1] or [Benefit 2]? If so then view my profile NOW.

~

Award Winning [Job Title] with [Years] Year's Experience, available NOW for top level assignment

~

Are you one of the [Extraordinary statistics] who suffer from [problem1] and are frustrated with [problem2] If so, contact me.

~

Proven [record/ability] to [action verb such as: Initiate, Innovate, Inspire] new startup technologies

~

[X] Years of experience as a [Job Title] who was responsible for [Role] on behalf

~

Click My Profile to Discover How I achieved [Achievement]

~

Client Admits [Embarrassing Problem] Because of [Reason]. Click my Profile to find out How Much Your [Embarrassing Problem] is Really Costing You.

~

Solve Urgent [Job] Problems. Engage me as your [Job Title].

~

[Your Name] is your ideal [Job Title] for 7 very simple, powerful reasons. Click His Profile to Find out More.

~

[Famous Brand Name] Gave me only [Timescale], to [Objective] and they were delighted with a [%] ROI.

 Pick 3 from the above list, and test them each for a week, to see if it helps to increase the number of profile visits and enquiries you receive.

Generating Referrals

Here's a wee bonus for you....

…It's a referral marketing system that you can use online and offline.

At the end of every sales appointment, 1-2-1, phone call or time when you have given value and service to another individual, use this simple 4 step script to generate even more leads and referrals for you, your products and services – It works, if you use it **at the end** of your meeting or interaction and <u>after</u> you know you have delivered or given value to the other party.

It's called: **BBRW** and can be used:

OFFLINE – At the end of your appointments, 121s and sales meetings

ONLINE – At the end of your website profiles, signup process, blogs etc.

MOBILE – Via SMS or SKYPE

You simply ask the following 4 questions to receive the referrals you want:-

Benefit – "Have you found a benefit from the time we've spent together? "

Benefit – "Do you think others could benefit from what I have to offer?"

Recommend – "Would you recommend me and what I offer to others?"

Who – "Who would be the first two people that you think could benefit from what I offer?"

For a short video tutorial on how to apply BBRW click the link below.

https://www.youtube.com/watch?v=DjOJhN6N36Y

How to prove to everyone that it's working

You need to monitor your investment in time, effort, energy and "opportunity cost". Far too many people don't set objectives, don't have a plan or worse – simply don't test and monitor the effectiveness of their social networking in commercial terms. No, they're too obsessed with being liked and creating an army of electronic buddies that are quite often needy, desperate & skint. As we discussed in part 2, you need to count, monitor & measure your progress regularly.

An essential part of prospecting, is monitoring your progress, against your objectives, and measuring what you have achieved against key mile stones – on a regular basis. You can measure your success/progress in a number of ways. Just remember, it all takes time.

If social networking on Linkedin.com were an Olympic sport, it wouldn't be a 100m sprint it would be a marathon. You need to prepare, you need to practice, you need to put in the effort in order to get the results, and it does take time. We also need to monitor our own performance and amend our activities. Use the activity sheet I shared in part 2, but also consider measuring:-

No. of views to your presentations and documents on Slideshare
No of profile visits
No. of contact requests
No. of Status Updates
No. of recommendations
No. of phone calls
No. of backlinks
No. of enquiries
No. of sales
No. of referrals
No. of appearances in search results
No. of signups
No. of downloads
No. of subscribers

Sometimes things don't go according to plan, or people fail to deliver on their promise for whatever reason. So we must ensure our plan stays fluid and can be revisited and adapted often. You'd be surprised how many people don't test new approaches, having found that the last one didn't work. We need to count and measure our progress then try different tactics and different approaches on the Linkedin platform. Think about alternating them each day, for example –

Mon. Writing a Status Update. Like and share other people's updates.
Tue. Uploading a document to Slideshare.net, like a group post, follow up your profile views
Wed. Write an article pingler it and share it on twitter, Google Plus & Facebook
Thu. Give recommendations to your existing network. Visit other people's profiles.
Fri. Connect with your 2nd & 3rd tier network and posting in different groups

Alternate your daily activities each week. Your time on Linkedin is all about testing new approaches, new groups, posting educational content and answering questions that helps to demonstrate your expertise.

Ensure you've got a well thought out content strategy for your Linkedin marketing activities.

And when you start getting active, you just don't know just how big your network could grow.

 Write down which key performance indicators you want to use to monitor your progress & return on investment from your Linkedin activities.

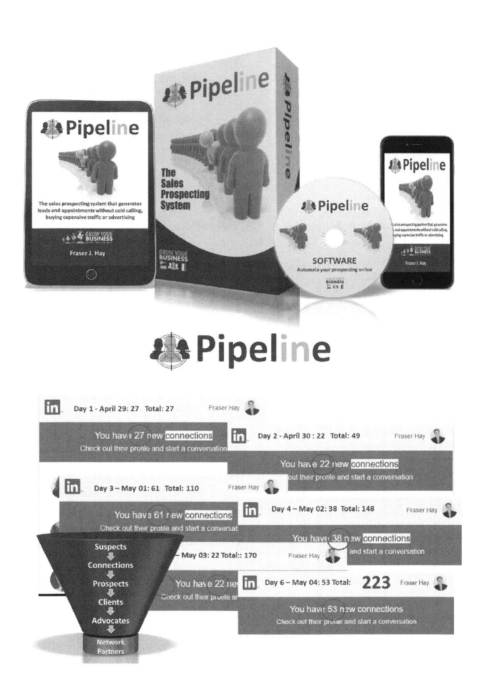

One Last Thing...

Have you found **value** and **benefit** from reading this book and in being introduced to different ideas to improve your prospecting?

Do you think others struggling with prospecting would find a **benefit** from reading this book?

Would you be prepared to **recommend** my book to others, or be prepared to write a positive review about it?

Who would be the first two people that you know who are self-employed or running their own sales team, that might benefit from reading this book too?

I really hope you have got value from my book. You definitely will if you choose to take action, and start making changes to your prospecting with the ideas and recommendations I've shared.

Take a moment, reflect on this book and write down the top 5 key "takeaways" you've gained from this book. Write what you've learned and consider adding a review of the book, for amazing things are about to start happening when you begin embracing and applying the principles contained herein, and my other books.

In addition to adding a review, consider sharing your thoughts via your online networks such as Linkedin, Facebook and twitter. If you believe the book is worth sharing, please would you take a few seconds to let your friends know about it? If it turns out to make a difference in their lives and businesses, they'll be forever grateful to you, as will I.

You can add your review by revisiting our product page in the Amazon Kindle Store.

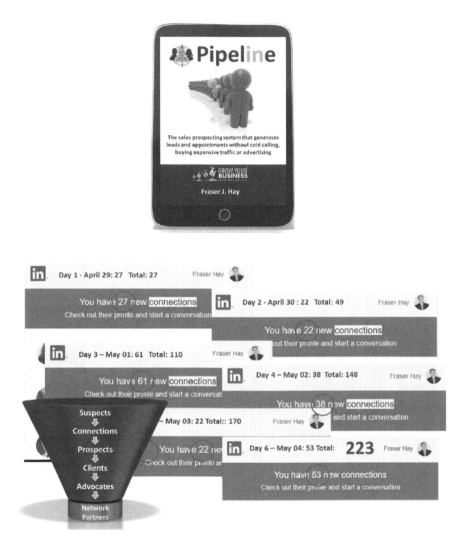

Part Four – A Thank You

Discount Voucher

TO: *You, valued reader*

FROM: *Fraser J. Hay*

AMOUNT: £100   REFERENCE: *PIPELINECOACHING*   TERMS: *One time use only*

GROW YOUR
BUSINESS

Bruntown Farm Cullen Moray Scotland AB56 4XD
WWW.GROWYOURBUSINESS.CLUB

Recoup a 900% ROI on your investment in this book by way of a discount voucher for the coaching program, when you contact the author– <u>HERE.</u>

Remember & Quote reference:
"PIPELINECOACHING"

About The Author

Unlike other IT, social media or marketing consultants, I approach marketing & GDPR Compliance in 2018 from a refreshing perspective of not just in becoming GDPR ready but in executing a practical plan of action that generates confidence, progress and results...

..Guaranteed.

• My latest book is called "Preparing for GDPR Compliance"
• All 15 previous books also got to #1 for their category on Amazon
• Pulled over 250,000 views to a blog in 24 hrs
• Generated as much as 236 leads on Linkedin in 24 hrs

Can I help you?
Maybe. Maybe Not.

YES, IF YOU WANT HELP TO:

• Make sense of GDPR & GDPR Compliance
• Document & Execute a NEW Marketing Strategy
• Hold your marketing staff, agency or VA accountable
• Fill Your Sales Funnel, Sales Pipeline with NEW leads
• Get GDPR ready & Grow Your Business®
If any of the above describe your current situation then imagine a few

weeks from now, experiencing the positive, permanent breakthroughs you or your stakeholders want.

Many small business owners are struggling to justify allocating human, technical or financial resources to GPDR Compliance without it translating into NEW leads, sales and revenue.

That's where I come in.

After all, Knowledge is NOT power. Applied knowledge is.

SOME QUICK FACTS

• Creator of the Pipeline Sales Prospecting System
• Author of "The Lead Generation MBA" Course
• Been featured on TV - twice.
• Over 400 testimonials on the UKs oldest social network
• A former Scottish & UK Shell Livewire, Royal Bank of Scotland & PSYBT Winner

I WORK WITH

• Entrepreneurs
• Business Owners
• C Level Managers
• Board Members

of

• Pre-start
• Start-up
• Small

• High Growth Businesses

In addition to getting GDPR ready, I can also assist you in EXECUTING a measurable, practical plan of action with full accountability & no excuses - ever.

Having explored my media section & profile below, claim your FREE "Instant Breakthrough" or for a wee chat, call me on +44 (0)1542 841319, email me or ping me via Linkedin.

My Linkedin Profile –
www.fraserhay.co.uk

Other Work by the Author

For more, visit: www.fraserhay.com

Made in the USA
Coppell, TX
29 February 2020

16310292R00076